WILD CATS
OF THE
WORLD

David Alderton

Photographs by Bruce Tanner

BLANDFORD

A Blandford Book

First published in the UK 1993
by Blandford, a Cassell imprint
Villiers House, 41–47 Strand, London WC2N 5JE

Text copyright © 1993 David Alderton

The right of David Alderton to be identified as author of
this work has been asserted by him in accordance with the
provisions of the Copyright, Designs and Patent Act 1988.

Photographs copyright © 1993 Bruce Tanner

Distributed in Australia by Capricorn Link (Australia) Pty Ltd
P.O. Box 665, Lane Cove, NSW 2066

Cataloguing in publication data for this title is available from
the British Library

ISBN 0–7137–2306–8

Typeset by August Filmsetting, Haydock, St Helens
Printed and bound in Spain by Gráficas Reunidas, S.A.

Contents

Acknowledgements

All photographs were taken by Bruce Tanner, except page 19 by the author, and pages 41 and 70 (*top*) by Graham Thurlow. The line illustrations were drawn by Mike Alderton.

Thanks are due to the many people who assisted in the preparation of this book, with a particular debt to the following:

Gaynor Worman, Marwell Zoological Park, Colden Common, Winchester, Hampshire.
Mike Lockyer, Terry Whitaker and Neville Buck, Port Lympne Zoo Park, Lympne, Hythe, Kent.
Mike Lockyer and Nick Marks, Howletts Zoo Park, Bekesbourne, Canterbury, Kent.
Alex Burr and Clive Barwick, Colchester Zoo, Essex.
Pat Mansard, Ridgeway Trust for Endangered Cats, PO Box 29, Hastings, East Sussex.
Bill Zeigler, Miami Metrozoo, Miami, Florida.
Terry Moore, Cat Survival Trust, Marlind Centre, Codicote Road, Welwyn, Hertfordshire.
Amanda Oxendale, HM Customs and Excise, London.
Denise Palmer for help with final picture selection.
Graham Thurlow.

In addition Rita Hemsley again managed to process my handwriting into a legible form, and Stuart Booth provided invaluable editorial support throughout the project.

Preface

Cats, the scientific family Felidae, rank as one of the most enigmatic of all mammalian groups. While we welcome the domestic cat into our daily lives as a companion, the lifestyles of many of the wild species still remain a mystery. In 1812, the noted zoologist Baron Georges Cuvier boldly stated that no other large mammals awaited discovery. Little could he have foreseen how, during the present century alone, three, and possibly four, hitherto unrecognized wild cats have been discovered, while reports of others continue to be made. The case of the onza reveals just how successful cats can be at hiding from people. Although documented by the earliest Spanish settlers in Mexico, who remarked on the appearance of these cats in the menagerie kept by the Aztec ruler Montezuma, it has taken over three hundred years since then for the first specimen to become known to science.

It is the larger species within the cat family – lion, tiger and cheetah, for instance – which tend to attract greatest interest. At the other extreme are those such as the kodkod and bay cat, which are known as little more than museum specimens.

Studying wild cats, especially the smaller species, can be a difficult and frustrating task. The application of modern scientific techniques such as radio-tracking devices has helped, but in addition to their secretive ways many wild cats are essentially nocturnal by nature. They also tend to occur at low population densities, so that obtaining an accurate impression of their numbers in a given area is not an easy task.

This raises particular problems with regard to the trade in their fur, which has undoubtedly contributed to the decline of some of the spotted cat species. Although trade in many species is already effectively banned under the international CITES (Convention on International Trade in Endangered Species) treaty, there still remains the spectre of illegal hunting. This practice will reduce fragile populations even further, possibly to the point of extinction in some areas. The impact of illegal trading is unclear, but according to recent investigations it may not be so widespread as had previously been believed. Allowing a very restricted off-take, or selling strictly regulated hunting rights, especially in the poorer areas of the world, can help to gain the co-operation of local people in protecting rather than persecuting wild cats that attack their farming stock. It is vital that the monies go back to the local communities themselves, however, rather than disappearing into a government's exchequer, if such schemes are to be credible. But while there is a possibility that some wild cats could be harvested for their skins on a sustainable basis, much more information is required about their population biology. In many cases, it is even unclear as to whether they have one or two litters a year.

Habitat destruction has now replaced hunting as the most significant threat to the survival of wild cats throughout the world, and is undoubtedly the major problem which will have to be addressed to safeguard their populations in the future. In many parts of the world where these cats occur, such as the rainforests of south-eastern Asia, the human population is still expanding rapidly, and land clearance for agricultural purposes or settlements is increasing at an alarming rate. Cats generally need large territories, because their prey occurs at a correspondingly low density. Setting aside relatively small tracts of land as national parks may not therefore be sufficient to ensure their survival, and is in any event likely to restrict their genetic diversity.

A particular problem is posed by the larger species, which may attack people. Frequent contacts increase the likelihood of fatal encounters, especially as the cats' natural prey also becomes harder for them to find in declining areas of natural habitat. The importance of barrier areas to keep cats apart from domestic livestock is becoming increasingly apparent as a means of avoiding confrontation.

But all is not lost, as I hope this book will confirm. Simple methods such as the wearing of a mask can lead to a dramatic reduction in attacks on people. Captive breeding is giving us a much greater understanding of the biology of wild cats, while their natural secrecy may mean, if only in some cases, that we have been unduly pessimistic about their numbers. There is also clear evidence that their numbers can regenerate well after a period of intense persecution, assuming that both suitable areas of habitat and prey remain available.

In the case of the cat family there have been additions to their numbers in recent years, rather than an immediate past littered with extinctions of entire species. The warning message is clear, however, since the range of many wild cats has contracted dramatically during the twentieth century and a number of distinctive races have already vanished, leaving others on the brink of extinction. For the latest news about their conservation you can subscribe to *Cat News*, the publication of the Cat Specialist Group of IUCN's (International Union for the Conservation of Nature and Natural Resources) Species Survival Commission, or the other groups involved in this area, knowing that your support will help to ensure their continued survival.

David Alderton
Brighton, England

While the large cats are well known, having captured people's attention, relatively little is known about the habits of many smaller species. This is a fishing cat (*Felis viverrina*), found in southern Asia.

Chapter 1
Wild Cats and People

The relationship between people and cats has always tended to be uneasy, oscillating between extremes of fear and affection. Even the domestic cat has undergone periods of intense persecution, being seen at certain times in history as an agent of the Devil, while larger species represent a much more direct and lethal challenge to human beings.

Our early ancestors knew and feared the cave lion, which used to be widely distributed throughout much of Europe. As a hunter, it represented a threat to human survival, frequently occupying the very places which offered them security. The cave lion was possibly one of the earliest victims of the ever-increasing human impact on the environment, and may well have been hunted into extinction. It was shown in a number of cave paintings before its demise.

HUNTING

The hunting of big cats has a long history and has always been especially popular among the ruling classes. The earliest records date back to ancient Egypt, to the Pharaoh Amenophis III (1405–1367 BC), who killed over a hundred lions in a ten-year period of his rule. Later, Assyrian rulers also hunted lions, pursuing them on horse-drawn chariots, although these particular cats were frequently bred specifically for this purpose.

Little could Landseer have foreseen when he incorporated lions into his now-famous landmark of Nelson's Column at Trafalgar Square, London, that about 100,000 years previously, cave lions lived in the area. This came to light when their remains were uncovered during building work here in 1957.

From ancient times cats have been admired and feared for their beauty and ferocity. Stamps, such as these from Laos, portraying the beauty of wild cats are common in countries that seek to promote their natural heritage.

The Romans organized hunting expeditions to capture wild cats and other beasts, and then had them shipped back to Rome to provide excitement in the amphitheatres there. Lions were often pitted against gladiators and used to kill prisoners in gruesome spectacles. Perhaps rather strangely, similar events also took place independently elsewhere in the world, reflecting the widespread fear which the big members of the cat family typically engender in people. The King of Pegu, in Burma, and Inca rulers in the New World regularly had prisoners killed by this means.

Yet it appears that the cats themselves did not relish the task, and may have had to be starved beforehand and then goaded in order to encourage their participation. A later revival of the Roman tradition resulted in disappointment for the voyeuristic inhabitants of Florence. They released twenty lions, alongside bulls and wolves, in their city streets in 1459. The lions did not attempt to fight with their supposed adversaries, but after an initial exploration of the area simply lay down to sleep.

A similar event, held in England in 1514, involved a greater assortment of animals and resulted in the deaths of three people. There was just a pair of lions on this occasion, however, which were set upon by dogs. Having killed two of the dogs, and dissuaded the others from attacking, the lions then carried on passively. They were finally encouraged to strike out by men concealed in large model tortoises and porcupines, who hit them with lances, but this also apparently provided no great spectacle to the onlookers.

International trade in cat skins has seriously affected the populations of some species, but such trade is now largely outlawed. This is actually a seized serval skin, confiscated by Customs' officers.

In more recent times cats have been hunted for their fur and as trophies, with serious impact on the numbers of some species, such as leopards. Such pressure, combined with loss of habitat, meant that by the 1960s these species faced an increasingly uncertain future, but since then growing and widespread public concern about conservation issues has changed the situation for the better.

Trade in cat skins is not a recent phenomenon, and it appears to have taken place in all parts of the world where wild cats are found. The earliest record of cat skins being used as clothing dates back to 6500 BC. At the site of Catal Huyuk in Anatolia, Turkey, archaeological evidence of dancers wearing leopard skins has been unearthed. The wearing of cat skins in such situations probably had a ritual significance. Aztec warriors often dressed in entire jaguar pelts, with the head attached and worn like a hood, while the tail was also left in place, hanging down the back of the wearer's legs. It was the cat's power, and its ability to remain unseen, that attracted these warriors to adopt its guise and thus, they believed, its nature. Elsewhere in the world, other cultures utilized cat skins in a similar manner. The Masai tribesmen of East Africa, for instance, adopted the lion's mane, while Dayak warriors on the island of Sarawak dressed in clouded leopard skins when entering battle. African chiefs and witch doctors frequently used cat skins as a means of emphasizing their authority over their people.

An extension of the cat's mythical properties resulted in the widespread use not only of skins but also of carcasses, especially in China and other parts of the Far East. The tiger in particular has been highly valued in oriental medicine for centuries. Most parts of its body have been incorporated into various potions said to cure a wide variety of ailments, ranging from heart disease to impotence. One of the most highly prized parts of the tiger's body is its whiskers. These are arranged in five rows, with those in the third row, which are normally the longest, ranking as the most valuable. The whiskers could be attached on clothes, or made into an amulet to wear around the neck, supposedly offering the wearer unparalleled power over women.

Tiger fat is also much sought after, with each carcass yielding on average 2–2.5 kg ($4\frac{1}{2}$–$5\frac{1}{2}$ lb). For centuries it has been made into balm and rubbed on to the body to cure joint and muscle ailments. Today this tradition continues, in spite of the fact that the number of tigers has plummeted. In addition, trade in tigers, their parts and derivatives should be strictly regulated under the Convention on International Trade in Endangered Species, best known under its acronym of CITES. Faced with a shortage of raw materials, however, manufacturers have simply resorted to using other products. Customs officials therefore find it virtually impossible to enforce the regulations because of the great volume of fake material being marketed. Steps to curb this and other similar wildlife crime have recently been taken by the United States government, which has set up a purpose-built laboratory in Oregon where accurate analysis can be carried out on seized materials.

In Africa, there grew up a belief that lions carried a stone in their stomachs which had magical properties but was rarely found, since the animal spat it out when it was about to die. Tribesmen would search frantically for this stone after a lion was killed. If worn around the neck it was believed to give them protection from dangerous animals. This story seems almost certainly to have arisen from the presence of hairballs in the stomach of some lions. When grooming themselves they will often swallow hairs, which may accumulate as a mat in the stomach. Here, in time, this mat can become impregnated with mineral salts, and ends up resembling a polished stone.

It is not only the larger cats which have been hunted for their skins. This Asiatic species, known as the leopard cat (*Felis bengalensis*), has been heavily traded for its attractively patterned coat.

Demand for traditional oriental products such as tiger balm remains a threat to tigers and other Asiatic cats, even if many such medications do not contain ingredients obtained from wild cats.

Trophy-hunting is now being turned to positive conservation benefit in some areas such as Zimbabwe, with hunters being willing to pay relatively large sums of money to kill individual cats. The money raised is then used to benefit conservation work in the area and the local community.

KILLER INSTINCTS

A number of wild cat species are known to attack people, but some strike with greater frequency than others. Lions will certainly kill humans, almost on a regular basis in some areas. Such an event was portrayed as early as 800 BC on an Assyrian ivory panel found at Nimrud. The most famous outbreak of this nature took place much more recently in East Africa, when the rail link between Lake Victoria and Mombasa was being built over the river Tsavo. The lions here began slaughtering the railway workers in 1898, and actually delayed the completion of the project for nine months.

Popularly known as the Man-eaters of Tsavo, these lions managed to kill twenty-six Indian workers and many Africans. Colonel J. H. Patterson, who was the engineer in charge of the project, then managed to shoot the two lions involved and wrote a best-selling book about the adventure. Nevertheless, sporadic attacks continued in the area. On one notable occasion a lion broke into a railway carriage and actually killed a police inspector who, with two companions, had been waiting to ambush it but had fallen asleep.

The reasons why lions become man-eaters is unclear. Although these were the most notorious, they were certainly not the only group attracted to the railway workers constructing lines across Africa at this stage. It does appear that the region around Tsavo had previously been frequented by man-eaters, however, possibly because of a shortage of suitable food in the area.

Another noted man-eating lion from this part of Africa claimed at least eighty-four victims during the 1920s in the vicinity of Ankole in Uganda. It is often the keen desire of a female with cubs to find sufficient food that triggers this reaction in the first instance. People prove relatively easy victims, and so seeking human prey can become a habit. Elderly or injured lions may also display similar behaviour for this reason.

The link between lack of prey and man-eating has been shown quite clearly in the Asiatic lion population. Now restricted to the Gir Forest region of western India, these lions used to prey to some extent on domestic stock but never attacked humans. Yet in just two years, after the cattle had been removed, this small population of less than 250 lions had killed fifteen people. There is no clear evidence to show that such behaviour is then more likely to arise in the future, as young lions reared on human flesh start hunting for themselves. But obviously it is a possibility, particularly if the environmental conditions have not altered.

Man-eating lions are remarkably bold by nature, entering dwellings in search of victims, usually at night. This unique predictability means that they are easier to kill than man-eating tigers or leopards, which can claim literally hundreds of human victims. Tigers are generally considered to be the most dangerous members of the cat family as far as people are concerned, sometimes attacking out of fear rather than aggression. When records of fatal attacks were maintained by the British authorities in India during the early 1900s, tigers claimed between 800 and 900 human victims a year on average.

The original European response to this situation was to hunt all tigers. This soon developed into something of a social spectacle, with rajahs taking their important guests out on elephants to engage in such slaughter. Native trackers called *shikaris* were used to locate the tigers on foot, and then a volley of shots would ring out from the so-called sportsmen, securely and safely positioned in the howdah on the back of an elephant, when the unfortunate cat ran into the open. Nets, traps, pits and poison were other less elaborate variants used by local people to kill tigers.

Some tigers gained particular notoriety as man-eaters, with the most deadly being christened the Champawat Tigress. She claimed an estimated 436 victims during her reign of terror, until she was finally shot in 1907 by the famous hunter Jim Corbett. He became a legend at tracking down and killing such cats, having learnt the necessary skills during his childhood in India. Corbett finally retired in 1938 at the age of sixty-three, on the same day that he had tracked and killed another murderous tigress without any help. In total, he accounted for big cats responsible for killing probably 1300 people.

Another of Corbett's kills was the so-called Panar leopard. Leopards are especially dangerous if they acquire a taste for human flesh. They will strike at any time, and show none of the natural fear of people which is displayed by tigers. In a number a cases this behaviour may be triggered, as mentioned earlier, by injury. The leopard of Rudraprayag had part of its left hind foot shattered. Even so, this did not prevent it from killing at least 125 people during its eight-year reign of terror in the vicinity of Garhwal. Corbett finally shot the animal, after a long period of tracking it, and a plaque was placed on the spot where the leopard fell.

The number of attacks by tigers has of course declined in the decades since then because of the plummeting cat population, but the increasing contact between people and tigers, as a result of habitat modification, means that there are still a high number of fatalities. In the Sundarbans mangrove forests in India and Bangladesh, for example, some fifty or sixty people die each year from attacks by tigers. The population of tigers here is known to be particularly aggressive towards people, and around a century ago the death toll averaged six hundred per annum.

A study carried out in this region during 1971 concluded that 3 per cent of the tigers here were dedicated man-eaters, while nearly one-third would attack people if an opportunity presented itself. Unfortunately this area is home to the largest surviving population of tigers in the world, comprising over five hundred animals. It has been suggested that being forced to drink saline water has resulted in the tigers' abnormally aggressive behaviour, because there is no shortage of other prey; but the construction of rainwater ponds has not significantly helped the situation.

Other practical measures have been introduced, however, to greater effect. Since November 1986 people have been equipped with face-masks – which are actually worn on the back of the head. This scheme is based on the idea that, since tigers invariably attack people from behind, they would be reluctant to strike if they saw a face.

At the start of this project, over 2500 of the 8000 workers visiting the area regularly, to fish or gather wood or honey, wore the masks. A year later, no attacks had been recorded on those wearing masks, but thirty people without masks had been killed here in the same period. Significantly, some of the victims had taken their masks off briefly, apparently encouraging the tigers to strike at this unguarded moment. Tigers were noted following mask wearers for up to eight hours, but never attacked.

There is always a possibility that these cats will gradually adapt their behaviour pattern and overcome their fear of the masks, but the Sundarbans region offers them a plentiful supply of other prey and so there is no immediate hunting pressure on them to adapt. In addition, pigs have been bred and released to provide an alternative food source. Another method, which also appears to have reduced human casualties, is the use of dummies dressed in worn clothes which have a human scent. If a tiger strikes, it receives a severe but not fatal electric shock from the dummy. Electrified fences have also been erected in some areas.

If tiger populations are to survive in the wild, effective means of managing them to avoid conflict with the local people is a priority, and this is nowhere more acute than on the Indian sub-continent.

Today the name of Jim Corbett, who in his time had to kill so many of India's wild cats, has been commemorated in the establishment of the Corbett National Park. Occupying an area of 521 sq km (200 sq miles), it is thought at the time of writing to accommodate an estimated 91 tigers and 47 leopards.

CAPTIVE BREEDING

As knowledge of wild cats and their populations in the wild has grown, there have been correspondingly important advances in terms of their captive husbandry. Zoos have developed a long way from simply displaying animals to meet the public's curiosity. The introduction of new construction techniques and materials has enabled the larger cats in particular to be displayed in far more natural surroundings, without the correspondingly stereotypic behaviour

Housing and feeding the bigger cats, such as this leopard (*Panthera pardus*), in zoos is a costly exercise but it allows people to appreciate the beauty of these creatures at first hand.

The difficulties of catching, shipping and quarantining cats can largely be avoided by the use of artificial insemination in breeding programmes. A puma (*Felis concolor*) is shown here.

patterns which could be seen in some individuals housed on their own in bare, barred concrete enclosures.

Much better co-ordination between individual zoological collections, reflected in the establishment of Species Survival Plans (SSPs), gives hope for the survival of many of the most imperilled cats, including Sumatran tigers and snow leopards. SSPs take an overview of the captive population, and every individual within it, with particular attention being given to the long-term maintenance of genetic diversity when arranging pairings.

In conjunction with this type of management plan, new scientific techniques are being employed to overcome the need to move cats for breeding purposes. Making cats travel may not only be logistically difficult and costly, but can also be stressful for the animal concerned, reducing the likelihood of successful breeding immediately on arrival.

The best-known use of biotechnology in the zoo field is artificial insemination, with sperm obtained from a male being used to fertilize the female at the appropriate stage to ensure conception. Such techniques are particularly appropriate in the case of cats, because females tend to rear their young entirely on their own and so the presence of a mate and father is not missed. Unfortunately, AI in big cats has not proved very effective, because of the need to anaesthetize the female. This appears to inhibit the movement of semen. More recently direct fertilization, using a laparoscope to introduce the semen to the uterus itself, has proved a much better option in trials carried out in domestic cats.

Zoo housing of captive large cats altered dramatically during recent years, and breeding, especially with some species such as lions, has become almost embarrassingly prolific. In some zoos population control is now necessary. These lions (*Panthera leo*) are at Amsterdam Zoo.

The other method is to remove the eggs, fertilize them outside the female's body, and then replace them. Breeding condition can be stimulated hormonally, and it is even possible to use semen from a wild donor, thus introducing new genes to a captive-breeding pool, without needing to keep the animal in captivity for any length of time. This *in vitro* fertilization method is already being used successfully in some zoos, and could be particularly valuable with the critically endangered Florida panther (see p. 146).

Since the sperm of wild cats will bind to the eggs of domestic cats, it is possible to test for fertility by assessing the extent of such binding. This is another useful development, as males can be assessed routinely to determine when they are mature, for example. Methods of saving precious genetic material in elderly cats, which may not even have bred themselves, are also now being developed. This will help to ensure that the widest possible genetic base is maintained. The ovaries contain far more eggs than are ever released during the cat's life. These can be matured artificially, and fertilized, before being implanted into a surrogate female.

The human race invented sophisticated firearms which were used to decimate tiger populations in India during the Raj, and developed heavy machinery to tear down their habitat across the world. It is perhaps ironic, therefore, that some people now query the morality of applying science and technology in this fashion to maximize the tiny genetic remnants of some wild cat populations.

There can be no doubting that captive breeding of wild cats can be very successful. This then creates problems, because these carnivores are very expensive both to house and to feed. Contraceptive implants are now having to be employed to restrict the breeding activities of some big cats, and euthanasia of litters is not unknown. Unfortunately there is not enough room in the Ark to accommodate all of them, which is why curbing habitat loss now is so critical if there is to be any hope of these majestic mammals continuing to roam free, rather than being represented in cold storage in genetic tissue banks.

Chapter 2
Form and Function

Cats have evolved into highly efficient predators, and this has resulted in a uniformity of appearance which is apparent in all members of the group. While there is an obvious variation in size and coat coloration between today's cats, there is no doubting to which family they belong. This similarity has, however, made it particularly difficult to unravel the relationships between them, giving rise to considerable taxonomic controversy.

HEAD AND SKULL
The shape of the skull is perhaps the most obvious feature. It is short and rounded, in contrast to that of other carnivores such as dogs, and this difference is a reflection of the different hunting techniques employed by cats. Although scent is important for communication purposes, cats rely to a much greater extent on their eyesight and hearing to detect potential prey. As a result their sense of smell is not as significant, and is less highly developed than in other predatory mammals. This is also reflected in terms of brain capacity: in cats the olfactory areas (the areas in the brain where the sense of smell registers) occupy just half the amount of space that they do in dogs. Even so, the density of receptor cells in the nasal passages of cats is significantly higher than in dogs, giving them greater sensitivity.

The cheetah has a longer skull than other cats, with greatly enlarged nasal passages. This seems to be for respiratory reasons, related to the cheetah's method of hunting, rather than being indicative of a different means of locating prey, based on scent. To run down game cheetahs rely on their pace, which creates a high demand for oxygen. They then suffocate their quarry by gripping the throat area, and so have little immediate opportunity to breathe through the mouth and overcome the oxygen debt which they have incurred. The enlarged nasal passages thus make it possible for these cats to inhale effectively at the same time as killing their prey.

Dentition
The shortening of the skull has led to a reduction in the number of teeth in the mouths of cats, compared with other carnivores. They generally have sixteen in the upper jaw and fourteen in the lower jaw, making a total of only thirty. In a few cases, such as Pallas's cat, the absence of upper pre-molars reduces this figure even more, to just twenty-eight. This represents a marked reduction from the modern cats' relatively unspecialized ancestors such as *Miacis*, which had forty-four teeth, and at least ten fewer than members of the Viverridae (civets), their closest living relatives.

The canines, at the corners of the mouth, are relatively large and flattened in shape, being used to seize and kill prey. It has been suggested that the precise

Irrespective of their size, all cats – species both large and small – show a remarkable similarity in appearance, which is a direct reflection of their lifestyles. This is the Asian race of the wild cat (*Felis lybica*).

shape of the canines relates to the favoured prey of the individual species of cat. These teeth have a very particular role, penetrating between two cervical vertebrae in the neck region, forcing them apart and rupturing the spinal cord to kill the prey animal.

While achieving a strike of this nature may seem unlikely, especially when battling with struggling prey, there is evidence to suggest that a cat does operate in this fashion – having seized its quarry, it takes care not to bite into bone. The number of mechano-receptor cells (cells which are sensitive to pressure) is highest in the vicinity of the canine teeth, and both sensory and motor nerve functions appear to be extremely rapid here, with the jaw muscles themselves also being unusually responsive. These factors all indicate that once the cat has gained a hold on its quarry it is able to use its canines to feel for the most effective position to bite and kill.

The risk remains during this struggle, or to a lesser extent when feeding, that the teeth could encounter bone. It is for this reason that the skull itself, and the muscles of the neck, are arranged to minimize the impact of such resistance, being able to absorb the resulting unexpected stress transmitted from the teeth.

The jaws are hinged so that movement in one plane only is possible, rather than lateral grinding of the teeth. This restricts the ability of cats to chew their food, but at the same time it ensures that the specialized carnassial teeth can function effectively. Formed by the first lower molar and the fourth upper premolar teeth, which have become longer and higher through evolution, the carnassials act like scissors, shearing through flesh. Cats' jaw structure is such that only one pair can function at any time, which is why they are often seen feeding with their heads tilted, using one side of the mouth only for this purpose, before swopping to the other side.

The canine teeth of all cats are well developed, being used to seize and then kill prey by severing the spinal cord in the vicinity of the neck.

The incisor teeth at the front of the cat's mouth are significantly smaller than the canines. A wide gape helps the cat to seize its prey effectively, as shown here in the case of the lion (*Panthera leo*).

There is a convenient gap between the canine teeth and the carnassials, which enables the canines to be sunk to their full extent into prey without being blocked by teeth immediately behind them. The siting of the carnassials is also significant: their location further back in the mouth, close to the powerful masseter muscles, enables them to be used for gnawing with maximum effectiveness.

The incisor teeth, at the front of the mouth, are small and typically arranged in a straight line, rather than curving slightly round the sides of the mouth as in most mammals. They help the cat to maintain a grip on its prey, so that the canines can then be used to deadly effect. After a kill, the incisors are used initially to pull off the skin covering of fur or feathers and later to strip off small pieces of meat adhering to bones.

While the carnassials in most species are able to crush bones, this does not apply in the case of the cheetah, which has exceptionally narrow carnassials. The unusual nature of the cheetah's dentition is further emphasized by the canine teeth, which are relatively short. These modifications are believed to be related to its hunting habits. By reducing the size of these teeth, the volume of the nasal opening, which is restricted by the size of the roots of the canines in the upper jaw, is effectively enlarged. The cheetah is therefore able to increase its respiration, which is obviously valuable for a species so dependent on its speed to obtain food.

Cheetahs have been forced to modify their killing technique because of the respiratory effort required to run down prey. The canines are relatively small compared to those of other cats and it is believed that they are reduced in size so that the roots take up less space in the upper jaw, thus leaving more room for a larger nasal opening which assists the cheetah when it runs at such great speed.

The cheetah's method of killing means that this reduction in canine size does not compromise its effectiveness in dispatching prey. The canines are used to suffocate quarry, rather than to rupture the spinal cord, which would require them to be longer. A study of the surrounding musculature reveals that the cheetah's gape is relatively small compared with that of other cats. This can be related to the roof of its skull, which slopes backwards from its highest level above the eyes. This in turn affects the arrangement of the temporalis muscle, which provides the force for closing the jaws. In other cats, these muscle fibres lie in a more vertical position. With shorter canines, this species clearly does not need to open its jaws as wide to inflict a fatal bite. As a consequence, the relatively horizontal positioning of the temporalis muscle fibres is not a disadvantage.

The temporalis muscle extends from the side of the cranium to attach to the special coronoid process of the lower jaw. While there is adequate space for attachment in smaller cats, the cranium is not large enough in the bigger species. This has led to the development of a sagittal crest, a raised area, at the back of the skull to provide a greater area for this purpose

The sagittal crest is clearly evident on the top of the skull of this leopard, towards the rear, as a raised area. All cats have a surprisingly similar general skull shape.

Cats have evolved the most efficient muscular combination for inflicting a lethal bite and then chewing the resulting carcass. The predominant muscle mass for this latter function, the masseter, attaches to the powerful and bowed zygomatic arch of the skull, and extends from here to the mandible.

Vision

All predators depend on an efficient sensory system, first to locate prey and then to be able to strike with lethal accuracy at close quarters. For this purpose cats depend primarily on their sight and hearing, rather than on their sense of smell. This is partly a result of their lifestyles, for the majority of species often hunt after dark when sound becomes more significant. In contrast, scent is widely used by cats for communication.

Cats' eyes show adaptations to nocturnal vision. In the first place they are relatively big, which enables the pupils to be correspondingly large. This in turn enables more of the available light to enter the eyes. But in order to be effective there must be a means of concentrating the light on to the retina, rather than allowing it to be diffused as would occur if the entire eye was simply enlarged. The cornea is therefore more sharply curved, as is the lens, creating a bigger anterior chamber in front of this latter structure. The retina is effectively positioned closer to the lens as a result, which ensures greater sensitivity to the rays of light impacting here.

The broad yet short head shape of cats is illustrated here. The eyes of cats are relatively large, in relation to the rest of their head size, emphasizing the relative importance of vision for hunting purposes. A leopard cat (*Felis bengalensis*) is shown.

The effect of the *tapetum lucidum* is clearly apparent in the case of this tiger (*Panthera tigris*), with light being reflected back from here to the retina of each eye, increasing its ability to see under conditions of low light intensity.

27

The retina contains two different types of cell, which connect via the optic nerve to the cat's brain. These cells are known as rods and cones; rods are more responsive in low levels of light. Rods predominate on the retina of most cats, but cones can also be found in the centre of the retina.

The cone cells can be divided into two groups, one of which is sensitive to blue light while the other responds to green, although the actual significance of colour vision to cats is not well understood at present. They appear not to rely significantly on coloration when hunting, and may only be aware of colours at close quarters. Investigations have shown that, through prolonged training, it is possible for domestic cats to learn to distinguish colours. The fact that such training is necessary suggests that they do not normally use this information. Colour vision in this case merely offers a means of seeing better during daylight – it does not have any real discriminatory function.

The nocturnal vision of cats benefits from the presence of the *tapetum lucidum*. This is not unique to cats, being present in virtually all carnivores, and is located behind the retina. Here it acts as a reflector, directing light which has passed through the retina back into this region, so stimulating the receptors again. It is for this reason that cats' eyes appear to glow when a light is shone on them in the dark, with the light being reflected back to the onlooker. Under normal circumstances, however, this does not occur because there is inadequate light at night. The structure and effectiveness of the *tapetum lucidum* vary from one group of mammals to another. In the case of cats it is highly evolved, consisting of as many as fifteen distinct layers of cells.

During the daytime cats must adapt their vision accordingly, and the structure of their eyes reveals much about their lifestyle. Species which are primarily nocturnal, such as the lynx, have a much larger anterior chamber to their eyes than others such as lions, which are active during the day as well as at night.

The amount of light passing through to the retina can be restricted by means of the pupillary diameter. Domestic cats' eyes are only slightly smaller than those of humans, yet they can increase their pupillary area three times more than we can, as well as reduce it further. This is largely because of the circular shape of the ciliary muscles which control the size of human pupils: they simply do not permit this degree of flexibility.

Small cats generally have an elliptically shaped pupil, however, with the ciliary muscle fibres pulling over each other. While this does not compromise dilation, it also means that in bright light the pupils can be closed almost totally, apart from pinpoints at the top and bottom of each one.

The pupils of bigger cats may appear rounded at night, but they too are in fact elliptical in shape, as becomes apparent during daylight. Where the number of rods exceeds that of cones, this restriction of the amount of light entering the eye is vital under such conditions if the cat is not to be dazzled. While the sensitivity of most cats' vision is unknown, work with domestic cats has revealed that they can see effectively when the level of illumination is just one-sixth of that required for vision by humans.

Leaping and an effective strike at prey call for highly accurate judgement of distance. This can only be achieved by the eyes working together, and cats have particularly well-developed binocular vision which is better for this purpose than that of any other carnivore.

Pupillary shape and diameter vary according to the species and the lighting conditions. Typically, the pupils are in the form of vertical slits in the smaller species. This can be seen in the jungle cat (*Felis chaus*) shown above, but can become rounded as in the fishing cat (*Felis viverrina*) shown below.

Hearing

The structure of the ear is one of the particular anatomical features of cats. The auditory bullae form part of the middle ear, containing the ear ossicles – sheets of tissue which vibrate in response to sound waves, and create what the brain ultimately recognizes as sound. The major distinguishing characteristic of the auditory bulla in cats and closely related carnivores is that it is partitioned, by a double layer of bone comprising ectotympanic and endotympanic components. In addition, cats also lack a major blood supply to this region, which in other mammals is provided by a branch of the carotid artery entering the skull close to the bulla in each ear.

Cats have an extraordinary hearing range which extends from 200 Hz up to 100 KHz, enabling them to detect sounds well beyond the hearing ability of humans. Yet at the upper end of the scale the practical limit is likely to be around 70 KHz, because the volume of the sound would need to be very loud to be audible even at this frequency. Interestingly, as in people, the ability of cats to detect high frequencies declines with their age.

The serval has particularly acute hearing, which helps it to locate small rodents in grassland where they could otherwise remain hidden. It is able to detect their ultra-sonic calls, which are inaudible to the human ear.

The sensitivity of cats' hearing can be related to their prey. Rodents, which comprise a major part of the diet of smaller species in particular, communicate with each other using ultra-sound, which is inaudible to human beings. The frequencies of rodent calls fall within the range of 20–50 KHz, which is well within the hearing capabilities of cats.

Such sounds as the noise of a rodent moving through grass are often of low frequency. In order to collect the sound effectively, cats have also evolved broad pinnae (ear flaps). Servals have the largest external ear flaps of all felids, to enable them to detect their prey which mainly comprises rodents. The pinnae are also mobile to an extent, but this does not convey the source of sound with precise accuracy. Indeed, the ability of cats in this regard is no better than that of humans. Even so, the shape of the pinnae can probably be related to that of the sound source, enabling the cat to learn by experience where a rodent is most likely to be hidden.

Particular problems may occur in deserts, where sounds are masked by the hot air. Sand cats not only have large external ear flaps, but also display a further adaptation. Their auditory bullae are enlarged, which may assist them in detecting specific vibrations. This is because the desert is naturally quiet, enabling specific sounds, such as those made by prey to be isolated more easily. The enlarged bullae, having less air resistance, are thought to allow the ossicles within to vibrate at these particular frequencies. A similar adaptation is evident in desert rodents, probably serving to alert them to the presence of a likely predator.

Sense of smell

It is generally agreed that cats rely less on their sense of smell than do other carnivores, certainly when pursuing prey. But smell is important for communication purposes. The area of the brain given over to olfactory stimuli is relatively small in cats, as mentioned previously. Yet cats, like other carnivores, possess a vomeronasal organ, which is a pouch-like structure in the roof of the mouth. It is lined with receptor cells, and positioned just behind the incisor teeth. While it has been suggested that this structure, sometimes also known as Jacobsen's organ, may have a role in stimulating gastric secretions, this explanation suffers from the fact that cats bolt their food down rapidly.

Its function may be more significant in intra-sexual communication. Male cats make a gesture known as flehmening when they smell a female's urine. They curl their lips upwards, baring their teeth, wrinkling their nose and raising their head. Such behaviour has been widely observed in wild cats, but is less conspicuous in the domestic cat where the Jacobsen's organ is relatively small. It is probably the means by which a male cat determines whether a female is in oestrus and therefore ready for mating. This information would be particularly significant in cats which tend to lead solitary lives.

The view that the vomeronasal organ is more important for reproductive than hunting purposes is supported by considering its inputs into the brain. It connects to the medial hypothalamus and the medial pre-optic areas, which are known to be involved with sexual behaviour. It also links to the ventral-medial nucleus, the part of the brain which actually causes the cat to cease eating, and does not share an association with olfactory input from the nose itself.

31

Scent molecules breathed in via the mouth will impact on the cat's vomero-nasal organ, enabling a male to determine when a female in the vicinity is ready to mate. This is particularly useful in solitary species like the jungle cat (*Felis chaus*).

Tongue and taste

The cat's tongue has a rough surface because it is covered by a large number of minute sharp projections known as papillae, which point backwards. They are sometimes arranged in a patch at the front of the tongue. These papillae are used in conjunction with the teeth to rasp particles of meat off bones by licking them. The tongue is also used for grooming purposes, and the papillae help to remove loose hairs from the coat.

Cats, unlike other more omnivorous mammals, are not well equipped to digest sugars. It is not surprising, therefore, that the cat's taste receptors respond in a different way from those of dogs, for example. They detect acid, salt and bitter tastes quite readily, but show a reduced sensitivity to sweet items such as sugar. Experiments have shown that cats tend to avoid such foods.

Tactile inputs

The head of a cat, like those of other carnivores, is equipped with specialist hairs known as whiskers, which have a sensory function. These hairs are normally divided into four groups, based on their position. Cats lack the inter-ramal whiskers, which are present under the chin in other families. This is probably because they do not lower their head to hunt prey by scent, relying instead on their vision and hearing.

Whiskers are clearly evident on the sides of the face in this Geoffroy's cat (*Felis geoffroyi*). In all cats these modified hairs playing a key sensory role.

The most important and well-developed whiskers in cats are the mystacial group, on the sides of the face. These can be kept extended, at right-angles to the jaws, typically when the cat is resting. As it moves forwards, these whiskers are brought forward and point more in the direction of the mouth. This is similar to the position adopted when the cat has caught prey – these whiskers help to provide crucial information about where to bite in order to inflict a fatal blow. There is now clear evidence that the whiskers and eyes can function together, complementing each other at this stage.

The mystacial whiskers also help the cat to find its way in the dark, when the fully dilated pupils make it difficult to focus on close objects. Cats which have lost their whiskers have trouble avoiding objects in their path at night. The whiskers' role in assisting nocturnal movement is emphasized by the fact that they are shorter in cheetahs, which are primarily active during the day.

This entire area of the cat's face is well endowed for sensory input: the skin between the whiskers also has separate receptors, which are very sensitive to pressure. It may not even be necessary for the whiskers to come into direct contact with an object, since they can detect the slight disturbance of air pressure as the cat passes close to objects. Anything which brushes these whiskers will cause the cat to blink, and so they serve to protect the eyes from injury as well.

There are further whiskers above the eyes, which may have a protective function augmenting those on the side of the face. Known as the superciliary

Winding its way through undergrowth, this Geoffroy's cat (*Felis geoffroyi*) can rely on its whiskers to give it sensory input about its positioning from its immediate vicinity, while it sniffs the ground cautiously.

whiskers, they are about twice as thick as the usual guard, or outer, hairs of the coat and are rooted deeper in the skin.

A third group, known as the genial whiskers, occur further back on the sides of the face, almost in line with the mystacial whiskers, but are probably less significant. There are other hairs on the body, notably at the back of the forelegs; these, sometimes called carpel hairs, are very responsive to touch. The tufts of hair present on the ears of caracals and lynxes are distinctive, but appear not to have a significant sensory function.

COAT

While the skin of cats is generally loose, minimizing the likelihood of bite injuries from rivals, the coat provides good insulation from the elements with a dense underfur beneath the outer guard hairs. This has enabled cats such as the snow leopard to colonize cold, bleak regions, while at the other extreme the sand cat also relies on its coat to help it survive under the baking desert sun.

Overall, however, the most important function of the coat is to provide camouflage, which is why cats generally display a range of spots, stripes and blotches set against a lighter background. These markings provide disruptive coloration, effectively breaking up the outline of the cat's body and enabling it to merge more effectively into its background.

There may be considerable variation in appearance between individuals within a species. Leopards which inhabit woodland tend to be darker in overall coloration, for example, with a more distinctive spotted patterning than those

Each species has its own characteristic basic pattern of markings in the form of stripes or spots, but within each species each individual cat is uniquely marked, like this handsome leopard cat (*Felis bengalensis*).

Tigers have essentially barred markings, being the only striped wild cats. There is again individual variation in their patterning, however, when they are seen at close quarters. A Siberian tiger (*Panthera tigris altaica*) is shown here.

found in open, arid country. A similar distinction can be made in the case of the European and African wild cats, depending upon their region of origin.

The snow leopard's coat is relatively long, with the hairs measuring between 3 cm (1.25 in) over the back and 6.5 cm (2.75 in) on the belly, which helps to insulate it against the cold. For this purpose its coat also has a dense and woolly texture, while the very pale coloration enables it to remain inconspicuous as it moves through the snow.

The lynx too has long fur, and in the far north of its range this cat undergoes a seasonal change in coloration, becoming lighter at the onset of winter. Its paws are well covered with fur to enable it to maintain a good grip when walking on snow. This can give the lynx a significant advantage when hunting prey such as deer, which are likely to have difficulty escaping through snow.

Interestingly, a similar technique has proved useful to the desert-dwelling sand cat. In this case, the fur covering the feet protects not against the cold but rather against extreme heat. These mats of hair, measuring about 2 cm (0.75 in) long, cover the pads and, by distributing the animal's weight more evenly over the surface, ensure that its feet do not sink into sand dunes.

Typically, cats' fur is longest on the abdomen and shortest over the back. Even so, seasonal differences may occur: the lynx, for instance, grows a longer coat over its hind legs at the beginning of winter. It is also not unusual for these cats to develop a longer ruff of hair around the neck, as do the bobcat and some tigers. But only the lion develops a full mane which extends from the lower part of the head to the upper back and encircles the neck as well. This is a secondary sexual characteristic, associated with male lions only.

The snow leopard (*Panthera uncia*) is one cat which occurs at high altitudes, where its dense coat provides protection from the intense cold, while its pale coloration helps it to conceal its presence.

Long tufts of hair on the ears are a feature of lynxes, and may serve to create a more frightening impression, deterring a potential rival when males meet. This is the Eurasian species (*Lynx lynx*).

The size, shape and colour of the lion's mane depend on the age of the animal and on the subspecies concerned. It starts to become apparent when the animal is about three years old, and is often of a yellow or brownish hue at this stage. Only as the lion grows older does it start to darken, and in time it may become completely black. Perhaps not surprisingly, lions inhabiting cooler, upland areas tend to acquire more profuse manes than those living in more arid, warmer regions.

An interesting case which confirmed the significance of a hormonal link in the development of the lion's mane was recorded some years ago from Nairobi National Park in Kenya. Here a lion with a magnificent mane had taken to killing lionesses, but rather than shoot the animal the park officials decided to castrate him. Within just three months of surgery the mane had been shed and he was indistinguishable from lionesses. Unfortunately the operation failed to subdue his murderous tendencies, and the wardens finally had to kill him.

37

The lion is the only species where there is evident sexual dimorphism, with the mane serving to distinguish the male from the female. This is controlled by sex hormones.

In addition to a full mane, male Barbary lions, which used to be found in North Africa (see p. 174) had a profuse tuft of longer hair extending from the neck along their underparts. This characteristic can be used to trace lions still related to this race, which is now extinct in the wild, that are seen in some zoos today. A similar feature was apparently also a characteristic of male Cape lions (see p. 174).

Unlike many wild cats adult lions, inhabiting fairly open country, have no body markings, and even a black mane blends in against this type of background. It is interesting that lion cubs usually have a spotted patterning at birth, however; the spots are sometimes arranged in lines, creating an impression of stripes. These markings may persist for some time, particularly on the underside of the body, and suggest that ancestral cats may have been spotted. As evolution has progressed, so the spots have been modified – into the tiger's stripes, for example, or essentially lost, as in the case of the lion.

The most marked contrast in appearance between adult and cubs is found in the cheetah. It appears counter-productive at first, since young cheetahs have long grey fur on their backs as well as dark underparts, which tend to stand out against the greenish coloration of the den where they are born. But it also makes young cheetahs look very similar to the offspring of the honey badger (*Mellivora capensis*), a highly aggressive member of the badger family. This provides an immediate deterrent to likely predators. As the cubs grow and leave the nest, their coloration blends in well against the grassland setting.

Variations in coat patterning of adult cheetahs have caused confusion in the past. For many years, following a paper given by a Major A. L. Cooper to a gathering of scientists in 1927 in which he described a unique skin obtained from

Most cats have markings evident on their coat. Lions (*Panthera leo*) have no obvious patterning, but typically have a dark tip to the tail, as shown here. This applies to both the African and Asian populations.

a cat resembling a cheetah, it was believed that this so-called king cheetah was a distinctive species. The key feature that distinguished it from other cheetahs was its pattern of markings, characterized by stripes running along its body and down the tail, with other, shorter stripes mixed with blotches on the sides of the body.

The skin had originally been presented to the Queen Victoria Memorial Library and Museum at Salisbury in Southern Rhodesia (now Harare, Zimbabwe) in 1926 by a farmer called Fraser, and was then sent to the Natural History section of the British Museum in London. Here, following further investigation, it was believed to have originated from a species of cheetah previously unknown to science. It was christened *Acinonyx rex* by Professor Pocock who worked there, in spite of his original doubts that it was simply an aberrant specimen of an ordinary cheetah.

Pocock's decision provoked controversy: some zoologists maintained the view that the animal was simply a cheetah with unusual markings, and was not worthy of classification as a distinct species. The suggestion was even made that the king cheetah represented evolutionary forces at work within the cheetah species.

This dispute was not resolved until the 1980s, largely through the endeavours of Lena and Paul Bottriell, who began their search for the elusive king cheetah in 1978 in southern Africa. They were able to document nearly forty specimens, and in May 1981 definite proof about the relationship of cheetahs and king cheetahs was obtained.

At the De Wildt Cheetah Breeding Station and Research Centre in South Africa, a pair of young cheetah cubs with the typical king cheetah patterning was born to normally marked parents. The mating had occurred by chance, from wild-caught stock which had originated in the northern Transvaal. The birth of these cubs provided proof that the elusive king cheetah was simply a variant of the cheetah. What is particularly interesting, however, is that, although slight variations in depth of coloration had been recorded in the past, no such clear change had ever been documented.

There is a highly distinctive difference in markings and coloration between adult cheetahs (*Acinonyx jubatus*) and their cubs, which is believed to assist in their survival.

The patterning of these two cats is remarkably consistent, but this is not surprising in the light of research which shows that cheetahs in the same litter show very little genetic variability. It now seems clear that the change in markings results from a recessive mutation, affecting the cheetah's tabby gene, being similar to that which creates the blotched or classic tabby patterning seen in domestic cats, where black markings are more solid in distribution and not spotted.

There are several features which distinguish these so-called king cheetahs. They have a longer mane and silkier hair, with their bold black markings set against an ivory or cream ground coloration. The tail is also ringed with dark markings and striped. The king cheetah, therefore, differs from all other wild cats which may show variation in their markings, because it is not just coloration or patterning which are modified but the actual appearance of the cat as well.

These cats were thought until recently to have a precise area of distribution, only occurring south of the Zambesi River. However, a cheetah skin confiscated from a poacher in eastern Burkina Faso in Central Africa in 1988 confirmed that this form occurred elsewhere in Africa too.

There is still the possibility that the terrain where king cheetahs are found can explain their appearance. Their main area of distribution is centred on an area which extends from eastern Zimbabwe down to Botswana and then along the Limpopo River as far as the Lebombo Mountains on the edge of the Kruger National Park. The Bottriells' investigations indicate that the border areas of Zimbabwe and Mozambique are the major stronghold of the king cheetah. In parts of their range, stretches of woodland and thorn forest predominate, which are also home to leopards. These cats are relatively arboreal in their habits and, being considerably larger, prey on cheetahs.

Cheetahs' (*Acinonyx jubatus*) markings vary noticeably through their range, and in open areas of grassland, when they usually occur, they are pale and lightly spotted, blending in against their background as shown here.

When viewed from above, the stripes running down the back and tail of the king cheetah provide additional camouflage. This may help to conceal them from leopards, as well as making them less conspicuous to possible prey of their own. There can be no doubting that the darker, heavier patterning associated with king cheetahs is more suited to a wooded environment. In other parts of the world, such as South America, forest cats with a similarly bold pattern of markings can be found: the kodkod is a typical example.

The actual status of the king cheetah remains something of an enigma, however, because although its markings are the consequence of a genetic trait it is not known how many 'typical' cheetahs possess the mutant gene. This is clearly significant, especially in view of the high mortality in cheetah cubs born in the wild, since relatively few will survive to become breeding adults.

Certainly, king cheetahs themselves are scarce. Yet it is possible that they mark a unique phase in the history of the cheetah. It could be, as zoologist Miklos Kretzoi suggested over fifty years ago, that they represent an evolutionary development. The cheetah may be starting to change its appearance, becoming better suited to a more sedentary lifestyle in wooded surroundings. Alternatively, in view of the rarity of these cats, it could be the reverse scenario. The king cheetah may be a relic of a time when southern Africa was colder and more heavily wooden than today. As the landscape changed, so the markings of these cats altered to that associated with the species today; but this transformation may not have been completed. In areas where the habitat is still suitable, cheetahs may on occasions regress to their former appearance.

What is clear is that a change has occurred primarily in a fairly localized population of cheetahs, near the southern tip of their distribution, while any

Melanism, illustrated here in the case of a jaguar (*Panthera onca*), results in an uncharacteristically dark coat coloration but with the markings still visible. Such cats will mate with normally-coloured individuals.

modifications to their appearance elsewhere in Africa, or indeed in Asia, are almost totally unknown at present. Further investigations may help to shed more light on this puzzling phenomenon.

Colour variations in other cats are not uncommon, and in some cases they have been sufficiently extreme to cause doubts over the identification of the species in question. The jaguarundi, for example, occurs in two distinct colour phases. This led nineteenth-century zoologists to recognize two separate species, identifying the red form as the eyra, under the scientific name of *Felis eyra*, with the blackish grey variety being recognized as the jaguarundi itself. It is now clear that these different forms can occur in the same areas, and may mate together, with young of both colours often occurring in the same litter.

A similar variation is known in the African golden cat, with some individuals also being more heavily spotted than others. These cats may also change colour, possibly depending on their environment or age, darkening in old age.

Occasional melanistic African golden cats have also been recorded – melanism is actually the commonest coat variant seen in wild cats. While the ground colour of the coat turns black or dark brown, the markings are unaffected, although they are far less conspicuous. It has been documented in no fewer than thirteen different species; according to zoo-based breeding studies it is often the result of a recessive gene. A notable exception is the case of the jaguar, where this has been shown to be a dominant characteristic, typically being apparent in the first generation of offspring.

After making a kill, cats will often carry off their quarry some distance before eating it, while the leopard, (a melanistic individual is shown here), will even drag a large animal up into the tree, caching it here, so it will be relatively safe from scavengers.

Of all cats, leopards are the most likely to show melanistic colouring, at least in the Asiatic parts of their range, where they inhabit areas of forest. Black leopards are less common in Africa, even in the equatorial rainforest. Yet the difference in appearance is such that they were originally considered to be a separate species and were christened 'black panthers'. It has since become clear that both normal and melanistic cubs can be produced in the same litter. There are no behavioural differences between them, although local superstition gave rise to tales that the dark form was much more aggressive than normally coloured leopards.

In contrast, paler mutations of some cats have also been recorded in the wild, in particular white tigers. In reality these are not usually albinos, with pure white coloration and red eyes; generally they have a lighter ground colour than normal tigers, of a pale creamy white rather than an orangish shade, and retain their darker stripes. Such tigers are best known from northern and eastern central India, where they have been recorded for over 160 years. Many of them have been observed in Rewa state. The Maharaja of Rewa started a captive breeding programme during the 1950s, and the descendants of these white tigers are now represented in various zoos around the world. A recent survey put their numbers at just over one hundred, and it is now clear that this white coloration is the result of recessive mutation

A so-called white tiger. These are actually just a paler colour variant of the Bengal race of the tiger (*Panthera tigris*), and not recognized as a separate subspecies. This mutation is best-known from Rewa state, India.

Why these tigers should have evolved in this region is unclear. They are simply classified as belonging to the Bengal subspecies (*Panthera tigris tigris*), and not given the status of a subspecies in their own right. Incidentally, although there have also been reports of melanistic tigers they remain elusive; only one confirmed sighting has ever been recorded.

A similar form of the condition known as leucism which gave rise to the white tigers of Rewa has been observed in African lions. Popularly known as the white lions of Timbavati, they were the subject of much publicity in the 1970s. Albino cubs had previously been recorded from the Kruger National Park in 1960.

LOCOMOTION: RUNNING, SPRINTING, JUMPING

The first investigations into the movement of cats were undertaken by Eadweard Muybridge, who took a series of high-speed sequential photographs for his book entitled *Animal Locomotion* which was published in 1887. The pictures revealed that cats move by using their legs on one side of the body first, and then the other. As they move faster, so they tend to start with their right feet, with the right

The cheetah's (*Acinonyx jubatus*) body is streamlined, being designed for speed rather than the athletic qualities necessary to climb trees.

foreleg followed by the opposite hindleg. Then, breaking into a run and using their hind feet together, they still place their front feet down in sequence.

To be an effective hunter, it is also important for the cat to be able to slow down rapidly in order to switch direction or come to a stop when it seizes prey. The limbs must be designed for running at speed, and yet also sufficiently powerful to overpower their quarry in the closing stages of their pursuit. These requirements mean that the cat's skeleton is reasonably generalized, although specialization is noticeable in the region of the feet.

The number of vertebrae in the cat's spinal column is remarkably consistent: there are seven cervical, thirteen thoracic, seven lumbar and three sacral vertebrae. Divergence from this pattern is seen only in the caudal vertebrae, which make up the tail. These vary from fourteen to twenty-eight, with the greatest number being present in cats such as the cheetah, which rely on their tail for balance. At the other extreme there is a noticeable reduction in tail length in the lynx, which typically uses its tail for communication only.

The structure of the limbs has become modified as a result of the way cats move. They are digitigrade, meaning that they walk on their toes rather than on the whole of their feet. It has proved possible for them to increase their stride length by a dramatic reduction in the clavicle (collar bone), which normally acts to strengthen the thorax (chest). In the case of cursorial species (those adapted for running), the stabilization provided by this bone, to prevent adduction and abduction (back and forth movement from the midline), is not required. By restricting the movement of the scapula (shoulder blade), the collar bone would also shorten the length of stride.

The scapula itself varies in shape according to the species. It is most elongated in the cheetah, with narrow and deep muscle attachments on its inner surface.

This contributes to the sprinting action associated with these cats. In contrast, in the arboreal leopard the area on the scapula where these muscles attach is shallow and broad, to assist in its climbing movements.

Relatively little specialization is evident in the case of the major limb bones lower down the leg, however, almost certainly because the cat has to face other challenges apart from running. It may have to climb as well as leap, in addition to overpowering its prey.

Considerable energy is expended in locomotion, and relatively long legs lessen the number of strides needed to cover the same distance. This is where the digitigrade stance is beneficial, because simply by lifting part of the foot off the ground – leaving just the toes in contact – the potential stride length is increased without adding unnecessary weight to the limbs.

In cats, the first digits on the front feet (sometimes called the dew claws) are held permanently off the ground since they are actually on the side of the legs. The equivalent digits on the back feet have been lost, but without compromising the cat's agility which is so important to its survival in the wild.

Increased stability in the lower limbs also helps to reduce the amount of energy expended when the cat is sprinting; not surprisingly, this is most apparent in the cheetah. The tibia and fibula bones in the hind limb have become joined by fibrous tissue, permitting very little flexibility in the vicinity of the ankle, with the tarsal bones below them also being fused. The situation can be quite different in arboreal cats, which require flexibility of the lower limbs for climbing purposes.

Cats are digitigrade which means that they walk on their toes, with the rest of the foot bones being incorporated into the elongated and flexible leg. A fishing cat (*Felis viverrina*) is shown here.

Some cats, such as the rusty-spotted cat (*Felis rubignosa*) will climb readily and can catch birds in trees. Their limbs are specially adapted for this purpose.

The most highly adapted in this respect is the margay, which lives in parts of Cental and South America. It is unique among members of the cat family in being able to climb down a tree vertically and upside down. Other cats crawl down the trunk backwards, before turning and jumping to the ground. The hind legs of the margay are particularly flexible: it is able to rotate its ankles inwards to an angle of 180°, which enables the cat to grab branches and hold on should it start to fall from a precarious perch. Its pads are also soft, which helps to absorb the stress of landing from any height.

All cats have a relatively flexible vertebral column, which enables them to swivel their bodies effectively during a fall so that they can land on their feet. The major risk to a cat falling from any distance is not so much limb injury as a fractured jaw. This is because the cushioning effect of the vertebral column between the front and hind legs does not extend so successfully to the vicinity of the head.

There is also another, less obvious advantage to having a flexible backbone. By flexing and extending the vertebral column it is possible to increase stride length. In the case of the cheetah, it has been calculated that this contributes about 70 cm (28 in) of its stride length of 6.9 m (22.6 ft) when it is running at a speed of 56 kph (34 mph), whereas the restricted movement of the scapula is responsible for just 12 cm (4.5 in).

47

Further specialization in the cheetah is apparent on the feet themselves. In other cats, when the claws are not required they are held by ligaments inside a sheath of skin. The claws emerge as the result of the combined forces of the lower ligament, which pulls the claws forward, and a straightening of the phalangeal bones joining the toes, which simultaneously pushes the claws in this direction. The claws are essentially protractile – in other words they stick out – rather than retractile, because no muscular effort is required to pull them back. The purpose of the skin sheath is to protect the claws from excessive wear; it also has the advantage of keeping the claws sharp for effective climbing – a skill not required by cheetahs. The curved shape of the claw does however force cats (except the margay) to move up head first and come down backwards, in order to maintain an effective grip for at least part of the distance. Since the cheetah has no skin sheath to cover its claws, they protrude beyond the fur. A similar arrangement is said to occur in the flat-headed cat.

However, even cheetahs will climb on occasions, and in some parts of their range lions may take to the trees as well. In Tanzania's Lake Manyara National Park the lions like to rest in the trees, seeking shade and a retreat from the biting flies. A tree also provides a convenient vantage point from which prey, otherwise obscured in tall grass, can be observed.

Leopards frequently take their kills up into trees, where they are less at risk of being disturbed by scavengers, including lions. Margays hunt regularly in trees, seeking birds and other small creatures, while jaguars may also lurk in the branches, dropping down and ambushing prey passing beneath them. They appear to leap not directly on to the animal's back, but alongside their quarry.

Claws are used not only as a means of seizing prey, but also to assist in climbing. They can be retracted in most species, with the notable exception of the cheetah.

The black-footed cat (*Felis nigripes*) has a reputation for ferocity, in spite of its small size. It hides away from larger carnivores in rocky outcrops and underground burrows, even termite holes, and emerges to feed on rodents and other small creatures.

Cats can prove patient hunters like this fishing cat (*Felis viverrina*) which, having chosen a suitable spot, is waiting for prey to come within reach. Hunting techniques must be energy-efficient.

Cats rely on their claws not only for climbing, but also for pinning down prey before they can subdue it. The cheetah's claws enable it to run at speed, gripping the ground as it moves, but this action tends to blunt them as well. This is why the front dew claws are particularly significant in this species, because they are not subjected to wear. Remaining sharp, and being especially well developed, they play a key role in helping to strike down prey in the first few critical moments of contact.

The claws are prone to injury on occasions, but if damaged they will usually regenerate. The cat can also sharpen them by scratching at the base of a tree or a similar object.

The feet are supported on pads, which help cats to move silently and effectively when stalking game. Even the first digit on each of the front feet has its own pad, although it does not make contact with the ground. These pads contain their own blood supply, and bleed quite profusely if cut. The cheetah's pads are tougher than those of other species, which undoubtedly helps them as they race across hard ground. They are also ridged, in a similar fashion to car tyres, which provides additional support when the cheetah is pursuing prey at speed.

But some cats do not need the element of speed to overtake their quarry. They have evolved a less active method of hunting, and jumping has become a vital part of their repertoire. This ability also enables them to be agile when hunting in difficult terrain.

The well-muscled hind legs provide the main thrust for cats, whether running or leaping. This is especially important for solitary hunters such as tigers (*Panthera tigris*).

Tigers (*Panthera tigris*) are not averse to water, and can swim quite effectively when necessary, crossing rivers in this fashion.

The proportionately longer hind legs of the puma enable it to jump nearly 12 m (40 ft) at a single bound – six times its maximum body length. Other cats may show similar agility: a snow leopard, for instance, was reported to have leaped a ditch measuring 15 m (50 ft) across when heading up a hill.

Tigers too are able to spring unexpectedly on to prey, covering distances of 10 m (33 ft) or more. This is a vital asset in a cat which preys almost exclusively on large mammals and needs the element of surprise when stalking them. Unlike tigers, lions usually hunt in groups; they are generally less able to jump, having relatively short legs compared to their body length. The maximum distance which they can cover in one bound is approximately four and a half times their body length – a distance of about 12 m (40 ft).

When jumping over an obstacle the hind legs provide the thrust, as they are the last part of the body to become airborne. The cat then stretches its body forwards as it comes to land, reaching forwards with its forelegs which absorb the initial stress of landing. The hind legs are then drawn in under the body in the final stages.

The body is also extended when a cat is jumping downwards, which in turn lessens the stress on the forelimbs when it lands. Initial contact with the ground is made by the pads, which act like shock absorbers under such circumstances. If possible, the cat will jump again using its hind legs to produce the thrust; this

The fishing cat (*Felis viverrina*) from Asia spends much of its life close to water, and will readily enter water to catch fish, hunting either in the shallows or swimming to reach sandbanks elsewhere.

should help to ensure that, although the forefeet were airborne first, the back legs land almost simultaneously, reducing the impact of the fall.

In addition to walking, cats may on occasion swim. Most species will only enter water with great reluctance, although tigers are certainly not averse to swimming and are capable of paddling along with their legs for up to 5 km (3 miles). Jaguars are also quite at home in water, and will catch fish and other prey in the shallows.

Probably the only species which regularly enters water is the fishing cat, whose distribution is centred on parts of South-east Asia where there is suitable shallow water. It normally wades into the water, but is able to swim when necessary. A breed of domestic cat known as the Turkish Van has developed a peculiar habit of swimming in Lake Van in Turkey, although it does not appear to hunt here at all. How this behaviour evolved remains a mystery.

CHANNELS OF COMMUNICATION

Although cats typically live solitary lives for much of the time, they have evolved a highly complex system of communication. This helps to avoid aggressive encounters and increases the likelihood of successful mating at the appropriate time.

It is not necessary for cats to come into direct contact in order to communicate. Scent marking will provide information to another individual about the cat's gender, its reproductive status, the extent of its range and its precise identity. This is particularly useful as cats may occupy relatively large territories at a low population density.

Cats in general lead solitary lives, and only lions will regularly associate in groups, called prides.

Cats rely heavily on their sense of smell to gain information about the world around them. Even wild cats can be very curious by nature, as shown by this bobcat (*Lynx rufus*), investigating the contents of a bag. Their stealthy natures mean that they can often escape detection in the vicinity of human settlements.

Cats use their waste products for repeated scent marking, enabling a relatively high density of signals to be established in a given area. Urine spraying is particularly favoured by both sexes: cat urine has a very strong and pungent odour. Prominent sites such as fences or the base of trees are chosen for this purpose.

The positioning of the male cat's penis enables him to spray urine effectively in various directions, so that it can be directed to a spot where it is most likely to be detected by other cats. The frequency of spraying appears to vary, depending upon the species and the gender of the cat. Male servals will spray as frequently as forty-six times in an hour, whereas females may only deposit their urine fifteen to twenty times during the same period. Some cats attempt to prevent their scent being washed away by rain by seeking out more protected localities for this purpose.

This may be reinforced with visual signals in the form of scratching on the ground to leave a distinct impression. Cats also have regular favourite scratching posts around their territories, which provide clear evidence of their presence. They also leave behind a distinctive scent, produced by glands between the toes. This is why they usually sniff at the spot first, presumably to see if any of their scent remains from the previous occasion.

Rolling around on the ground, this lynx is depositing scent from glands on the sides of its head, which will alert any other cats in the vicinity to its presence here.

Glands surrounding the anus leave their mark on faecal deposits. The significance of this method of communication probably varies between species, however, because members of the genus *Felis* usually bury their faeces in contrast to the habits of the larger *Panthera* species. An interesting variation on this behaviour pattern has been observed in the European wildcat. These cats deposit their faeces above ground at the border of their territories, often in exposed positions such as on a tree stump. Elsewhere in their range, their faeces are buried.

Cats also use scent glands on other parts of their body to mark their territories. There are a number of sebaceous glands on the cat's head; those on the chin are often used to mark objects – the cat rubs its face against them to deposit its scent. Familiar cats will mark each other in a similar fashion, rubbing faces when they meet, to reinforce the bond between them. Neck rubbing is also observed on occasion, but it is not clear whether this results in a transfer of scent. The scent from the tail gland is also used for this purpose, perhaps most obviously in domestic cats which rub themselves against their owners' legs.

Another response to scent is flehmening, as described on p. 31. Certain scents appear to elicit a particularly marked response in some individuals: catnip (*Nepeta cataria*) is well known among pet owners for its abilities in this respect. Wild cats, including lions, jaguars and snow leopards, react in a similar fashion when exposed to this plant. It appears that the presence of a dominant gene is necessary to enable a cat to detect the odour of catnip.

Catnip evokes a response similar to that of a female in oestrus, although both sexes are affected. The active ingredient of catnip is cis, trans-nepetalactone, which is thought to resemble an odour which cats themselves produce. Other plants, such as *Actinidia polygama*, can induce a similar effect. The concentration of the active ingredient does not need to be high – a level of one part in ten will produce a reaction in a sensitive individual.

A detailed study of scent marking has been carried out in the Royal Chitwin National Park in Nepal. Spraying urine was shown to be by far the most important method. It was also more persistent than other methods such as scraping, since the scent lingered for as long as three weeks. Tigers have evolved a loose hierarchical system of territories, with the male roaming through several smaller female territories. Yet scent marking is not confined to the male – the females are equally concerned about marking the borders of their territories. The study in Nepal found that, although females did not visit their borders more regularly than elsewhere in their range, they did spray here noticeably more frequently. When a newcomer arrives, the level of scent marking often shows a dramatic increase along existing borders. Similarly, when a female is ready to mate urine spraying is carried out with greater frequency, presumably to attract a male, who responds in identical fashion to alert the female to his presence.

A more transient form of communication is provided by vocalization, and in this respect there is a significant difference between large and small cats. It relates to the anatomy surrounding the voicebox or larynx. In members of the genus *Panthera*, the hyoid apparatus linking the larynx to the skull is partially composed of cartilage, creating a more flexible arrangement. This is said to account for the fact that these bigger cats can roar.

In comparison, *Felis* species have a bony hyoid, which allows less movement and has traditionally been thought to restrict their vocal range to that of purring

Roaring is a means of communication used in the larger cats, like this jaguar (*Panthera onca*). Unlike their smaller relatives, the *Panthera* cats are unable to purr.

rather than roaring. An interesting fact is that cats can purr continuously, while they are breathing both in and out, and may make this sound consistently for quite long periods. Purring is typically associated with a mother and kittens, and appears to indicate contentment. It is a low-intensity sound, and inaudible from any distance, thus helping to conceal the presence of young. The mechanism underlying purring is not clearly understood, but it seems likely that membranes adjacent to the vocal cords themselves are involved.

Three other different types of call, all of which last for under half a second, have been identified as being used for close communication. Other sounds such as meowing may be more general, and within a species these calls usually differ in their intensity and frequency as well as their duration.

Studies suggest that there may be between six and a dozen different types of call common to the repertoire of all cats, with each species having additional specific vocal sounds. These fall within a frequency range of 50,000–10,000 Hz, with the majority falling in the middle of this band.

Much still remains to be learnt about vocal communication in cats; however it is clear that they do not rely on their calls to harass possible quarry, as used to be believed in the case of the lion's roar. This is the loudest sound uttered by any cat, measuring up to 114 decibels. Roaring links the members of a pride, as well as strengthening their claim over their territory and deterring possible intrusions by neighbouring prides.

The ears of the cats are well-positioned to locate sound, and their positioning can be adjusted by muscles. This is not only useful for hunting, but also for communication between individuals at close quarters as in the case of this Eurasian lynx (*Lynx lynx*).

The white spots are clearly visible on the backs of this tiger's (*Panthera tigris*) ears.

This caracal (*Lynx caracal*) is behaving in a characteristically aggressive manner, by baring its teeth, with its ear tufts serving to intensify this threat gesture.

In most situations, however, vocalizations are used to communicate with other cats at close quarters. A range of specific mating calls have been identified in both sexes. There are also antagonistic calls, such as hissing, which if the opponent does not back down may build up to a crescendo and terminate in spitting. By this stage body language is also involved.

The ears have a vital role in visual communication. It is not uncommon for pale areas to be apparent towards the rear of the ears of many cats. These so-called 'eye spots' become particularly apparent when the cat moves its ears, either in a gesture of appeasement to a potential rival or to indicate a combative approach.

Under normal circumstances the ears are held erect and directed forwards. When challenging a rival, a cat moves the backs of its ears forwards and shifts its weight to its front feet, in a move designed to intimidate its rival. It also moves its tail rapidly from side to side. In the lynx, the ear tufts fulfil the function of the tail, which is shorter than in other cats. The markings here may also serve to emphasize the cat's aggressive nature at this stage, as does the accompanying low, growling sound.

Its opponent may respond by flattening its ears as a sign of submission. This occurs in stages, as each cat takes stock of the various signals given off by the other. Through this ritualization of conflict it is often possible to avoid actual bloodshed: the weaker individual will simply back off and save both cats from the risk of serious if not fatal injury. The pupils of the submissive cat become more dilated in response to the threat gesture as it sinks lower towards the ground. With its tail held low the cat will slowly slink off, sometimes being pursued for a short distance by its rival.

Encounters of this type may occur regularly in the case of social cats, notably lions, when a rival challenges the established dominant male. If actual fighting does break out it is accompanied by further vocalizations until one of the combatants retreats, often showing signs of injury as a result of the encounter.

TERRITORIAL FORCES

While the majority of cats live independently and come together only to mate, the concept of them living solitary lives is rather misleading. They are in touch with other members of their species through communication based on scent, sound and sight. But only three species, notably the lion, have evolved some sort of social organization. It appears to be related to food supply, with prides in some areas being noticeably larger than in others. Where prey is plentiful, and relatively large, it is possible for lions to hunt co-operatively and receive individual benefits. Yet this may be counter-productive in some cases. A more recent explanation suggests that, since prey stealing is so common among lions, it may be advantageous to restrict it to members of a group who, by hunting collectively, are likely to obtain more food than a solitary individual.

The highest number of lions living together in prides can be found in East Africa, where there may be between two and five males, and between five and twenty females and cubs. At the other extreme, in the desert areas of northern and south-western Africa, where prey is scarce, lions are more likely to be found in individual pairs.

When not hunting, cats often spend much of their time asleep or resting – like this serval (*Felis serval*).

The number of lions living in a pride is affected directly by the available food supply. Where food is scarce, only individual pairs may be seen. In a pride it is the lionesses (shown here) which usually hunt, rather than male lions.

Asiatic lions too occur in groups, rather than living on their own on a regular basis. An interesting insight into the social life of cats has come from observations of tigers in Ranthambhore National Park in India. Although it had long been assumed that tigers never lived together, this has been disproved here. These cats specialize in hunting large prey such as buffalo, and rely on an element of surprise in tackling what is a dangerous quarry. Given the lack of cover in the area of the park where they were seen, it was probably safer for the tigers to hunt in a group. Lions may have associated in prides for the same reason.

Male cats may live together in groups, sometimes known as coalitions. This is common among lions and also occurs in cheetahs, where two or three males may join up and establish a territory. Other males are driven away determinedly, and risk being killed if they persist.

The advantages of this social system revolve around the likelihood of obtaining regular food, which is increased under these circumstances. Such cheetahs are in better condition than those living solitary lives, weighing on average about 10 kg (22 lb) more and having a longer life expectancy, even though they do not necessarily mate more frequently. Only if there is a shortage of prey or water is the territory likely to be abandoned.

Studies of feral domestic cats suggest that adaptability to the local conditions is the dominant factor influencing whether the cats live socially or separately. Where food is plentiful females will often congregate together, while males are still solitary and roam further afield to seek out other mates. In contrast, on the island of Heisker, to the west of the Hebrides off Scotland, there is little for the cats to eat other than rabbits, which are scarce. As a result they do not share food and both sexes live on their own, rarely coming into contact with other cats, except for mating purposes.

Chapter 3
Reproduction

COURTSHIP AND COMMUNICATION

Since the majority of cats lead solitary lives, difficulties could arise during the breeding period. Most female mammals have a regular cyclical breeding pattern, ovulating at a set time within this cycle. Clearly this could have a considerable drawback for cats, in that the female might not have found a mate by this stage.

In the wild, cats roam over large areas. Although the territory occupied by a male may encompass that of several females, sexual encounters need to be carried out with caution if they are not to result in displays of aggression or even fighting. Cats therefore rely heavily on scent to initiate the mating process.

From a safe distance, the male will be able to determine the reproductive state of a potential partner. This is where the behaviour known as flehmening becomes particularly significant. The cat will pause and sniff at the urine, leaving the jaws apart. The upper lip is pulled back slightly in smaller species, and in a more pronounced fashion in the large cats. The cat is actually collecting scent droplets on its tongue, and then drawing them into its mouth. Here they come into contact with the vomero-nasal or Jacobsen's organ. Chemical messengers

This male African golden cat (*Felis aurata*) bears the scars of battle, evident by the injuries to the ears. These may have been received in fights over mating, being inflicted by rivals, in the same way that domestic tom cats fight.

Female cats will often adopt a playful posture when they are ready to mate, signalling their acceptance to the male. Repeated mating during this phase, sometimes with more than one partner, is common. This is a female leopard (*Panthera pardus*).

known as pheromones indicate the female's receptivity. The significance of this scenting method in the breeding behaviour of cats is shown by the fact that males flehmen far more often than females.

In addition, as they approach oestrus female cats start to spray urine much more frequently as they move through their range, in the hope of attracting a mate. Males respond in a similar fashion, presumably as a means of deterring possible intrusions into their territory by neighbouring males.

Sex hormones are present not only in the female's urine, but also in her body secretions. A female will rub herself around trees, often using her head to deposit traces of saliva which will attract a mate. Tail glands fulfil the same function.

There is a remarkable similarity in courtship between all members of the cat family, both large and small. The female will become sexually attractive before she is ready to mate, and may call loudly, encouraging several males to pursue her. This will almost invariably lead to fighting, which can result in serious, if not fatal, injuries, especially as males are often reluctant to back down under these circumstances.

In the case of lions, aggression may also break out within members of a pride which contains more than one male. The dominance hierarchy is more firmly established here, however, with a correspondingly reduced risk of serious fighting. The fact that most females in a pride come into oestrus at about the same time means that there is likely to be less friction within the overall group. In addition, a lioness may ultimately mate with several lions in the pride and not just a single individual.

Once a male has located the female, she is unlikely to be immediately receptive to his advances. Indeed, she may respond by lashing out at him, forcing him to withdraw. At this stage the male may use vocalizations to entreat the female to accept him, but will not advance significantly towards her.

Gradually, after perhaps several days, the female's behaviour begins to change and she may start to encourage his advances, responding to his calls and allowing him to sniff at her anogenital region. She often rolls on the ground during this pro-oestrus period, yet still strikes out with her paw if the male moves too close.

The function of this prolonged courtship is unclear. Where solitary cats are concerned, it may ensure that only the dominant male from the area is ultimately able to mate, having driven off his rivals – although sometimes a female may mate with more than one partner. There may also be a longer-term benefit, in that the male is less likely to harm his own cubs if he remains in the area, although this is not entirely certain in the case of most cats.

Nevertheless it is known that a newcomer, having displaced the resident male in a pride, probably kills any young cubs. Such behaviour will cause the female to revert to oestrus more quickly, enhancing the likely reproductive success of this new dominant male. Similar outbreaks of infanticide have been occasionally documented in other species, such as ocelots, pumas and tigers, but the circumstances are less clear-cut.

MATING

The majority of female cats are believed to be induced ovulators. This means that the ova are only released from the ovary in response to the direct stimulus of mating. The advantage of this reproductive method for predominantly solitary animals is obvious: it means that ovulation takes place when there is the greatest likelihood of fertilization occurring.

When the female is ready to mate she will adopt a characteristic posture, called lordosis, which enables the male to penetrate successfully. She raises her hindquarters, adopting an otherwise crouched posture, with her tail directed to one side. The male approaches, perhaps somewhat cautiously in the first instance, and may grip on to the fur at the back of her neck with his teeth. If necessary, he will use his hindlegs to tread over her hindquarters to induce lordosis before intromission occurs.

The penis, as with most carnivores contains a bone known as the bacula which stimulates the vaginal walls. Cats also possess erectile spines on the penis itself, which are thought to provide a further stimulus to ovulation. It is popularly believed that on withdrawal the female will cry out in pain, but this does not appear to be so. Indeed, having accepted the male the female will mate with him repeatedly – up to a hundred times a day in the case of leopards and lions. This frquency would be most unlikely if each experience resulted in pain.

The oestrus period may last for up to a week, with the frequency of mating being maintained during this period. By mating repeatedly, the cats are increasing the likelihood of ovulation and fertilization; a single mating may not prove sufficient.

Generally, smaller cats such as the ocelot, as well as the cheetah, mate far less often than their larger relatives, presumably because this would leave them

The breeding period of wild cats such as the Eurasian lynx (*Lynx lynx*) shown here, which occur in temperate areas is more restricted than for those living in the tropics.

vulnerable to predation by other carnivores. Their period of oestrus also tends to be shorter, lasting for just one and a half days in the case of the black-footed cat, although in cheetahs it may range from five to fourteen days.

In northerly latitudes, where seasonal changes may be highly significant, cats tend not to be induced ovulators. The breeding season of both the Canadian lynx and the bobcat, for example, is clearly influenced by the availability of prey. It is possible that when snowshoe hares, the main food item of the Canadian lynx, are numerous, the females ovulate regularly; but when food is scarce they become induced ovulators. There may also be variations between individual populations, which have yet to be appreciated.

A subtle alteration can also become apparent during the mating period, with the male progressively losing interest to the extent that the female has to take the initiative. This declining response on the part of the male is advantageous, however, in that it enables the female to seek out other partners with less risk of an aggressive response from her previous mate. In this way it is possible to maximize the likelihood of a fertile union during her period of oestrus, having given the dominant male the greatest opportunity to extend his influence to the next generation.

Indeed, the overall mating process of cats appears to have evolved to minimize the risk of serious conflict between the participants. The female only allows a close approach when she is ready to mate. It is exceptionally rare for a male to attempt to force himself on a reluctant female, and it would be almost impossible

A female tiger is pursued by a potential mate. The mating of big cats is carefully structured, to avoid aggression.

for penetration to occur without her co-operation. The mating position itself is distinctive, and could not be confused with prey capture. The immobility of the female during the process also ensures that the wrong visual signals are not given to her mate.

For his part, the male is forced to support his weight on his forelegs, while treading the female, with no pelvic grip. This position makes it impossible for his powerful limbs to be used in what could be construed as an aggressive manner. Further evidence of the way in which potential threat gestures may be removed from the mating behaviour of cats is seen in the larger species.

Male lions and tigers, for example, do not necessarily engage in a neck bite when they first mount their mate; they grip her only when they ejaculate. As a result, the female is likely to feel less threatened, which may have the effect of encouraging ovulation. Conversely, under conditions of stress, the possibility of ovulation is likely to be significantly reduced.

GESTATION, BIRTH AND THE NEWBORN LITTER

Following the end of oestrus the cats will separate, with the exception of the lion, and the male will take no further part in the reproductive process. The length of the gestation period itself is influenced by the size of the cat, being correspondingly shorter in smaller species. It typically varies from just 56 days in the African wild cat up to 114 days in the case of the lion.

Remaining within her territory, the female cat will seek out a suitable den where she can give birth to her litter in safety. The site chosen varies according to the terrain. Cheetahs, for example, may select a thicket, while European wild

The European wild cat (*Felis silvestris*) has a relatively short gestation period of about eight weeks, whereas a lioness carries her cubs for sixteen weeks before giving birth.

cats might retreat into a rocky den. Seclusion, together with protection against the elements and predators, appear to be key factors.

In the early stages of pregnancy the foetuses develop without the female gaining much body weight. This is especially important for the cheetah, as it would inevitably slow her down, reducing her hunting ability, at a time when maintaining food intake is vital for the development of her offspring. The major growth phase of pregnancy occurs during the last third of the gestation period. The cat herself may lay down more body fat, which can subsequently be utilized during the demanding period of lactation.

The kittens (offspring of the smaller species) or cubs (those of larger cats) may number between one and seven. Litter size is not directly related to that of the species. Some smaller cats, such as the margay, may produce a single offspring, whereas both cheetahs and domestic cats can have seven or more. The number may relate to the survival rate of the offspring, and possibly also to the availability of food during the pre-oestrus period.

All young cats are born in a dependent state, described as semi-altricial, with their eyes closed. This is not to say that they are unaware of their surroundings, because all the littermates soon establish a teat order. Most females possess double the number of teats compared with the likely number of offspring, and each young cat will develop the habit of suckling from one particular nipple. This behaviour avoids any potential conflict, which could result in a nipple becoming damaged. Early suckling is vital: during this period they receive colostrum or 'first milk', with its immunoglobulins which help to provide protection from infection until their own immune systems are fully functional.

Cats' milk has a relatively high level of protein. This may be a reflection of their diet, whose protein content averages around 10 per cent. Fat content would seem to be much more variable, depending on the species. It ranges from about 6 per cent in the case of the European lynx and the leopard, up to 9 per cent in the cheetah, and tops 18 per cent in lions and pumas. It has been suggested that this high level of fat may serve as an additional source of energy for the young cats while their mother is away hunting. The fat could be metabolized to help maintain their body temperature in her absence. However, this explanation is not universally accepted.

During the first couple of days after giving birth the female cat remains very close to her offspring. They may suckle for eight hours or more. Milk-treading is widespread in members of the Felidae. The kitten pushes against its mother's body, close to the teat, using its front paws alternately. The effect is to stimulate the flow of milk.

If their mother disturbs the feeding kittens by moving away at this stage they may cry out, especially if one of them is carried away from its littermates by her movement. Should a kitten end up just a short distance away, however, it may well be able to crawl back by itself to the warmth of its siblings.

It is not unusual for the female to move her offspring to another den, especially if the area is relatively exposed. Cheetahs have been known to change the location of their cubs twenty times over a period of just six weeks. Each cub needs to be moved individually, being carried by the scruff of its neck in its mother's mouth. This method is also used if a youngster strays too far from the protective eye of its parent.

The young cats will be born in secluded surroundings, with many species such as the bobcat (*Lynx rufus*) giving birth to their young in a den, where the cubs can remain hidden.

Cheetahs may prove to be amongst the most prolific of all wild cats, sometimes giving birth to seven cubs or more, but mortality can be high in this species.

The female helps to keep the youngsters warm at first, remaining with them for most of the time. By licking them all over she not only keeps them clean but also encourages urination and defecation. Their excreta is consumed by her, which keeps the den relatively clean and dry. It also prevents the build-up of any odour, which could betray their presence to potential enemies.

Kittens are generally quiet in the den, and only vocalize if they are in some way uncomfortable or short of food. Clearly, by calling out frequently they could alert predators. They will often purr quietly, however, in the case of the smaller species and particularly while they are suckling, which provides support for the theory that purring is a sign of contentment.

As her offspring grow, so do the demands on their mother. It is not unusual for a female cat to lose weight and condition while suckling, as her body reserves of fat are converted to provide the energy input required by her kittens. Large litters not only develop more slowly in terms of body weight gain, but are also weaned earlier, emphasizing the strain of the lactation period.

Cats face a particular problem in that, with the notable exception of the lion, the female not only has to care for the young but also to find and catch sufficient food for the family. Within a couple of days she will be forced to leave her offspring to search for prey, returning at intervals to allow them to suckle from her. She will go to considerable lengths to conceal her presence and that of the den at this stage, burying her faeces and disguising her urine. Apart from threats posed by other species, there is always the risk that a male cat in the vicinity may be attracted to the den and kill the young.

The availability of food may be one of the factors which influence a female cat when she is choosing the site for her den. Certainly she may stay much closer than under normal circumstances, returning to the den frequently during the day and

Most cats rest during the day, becoming active towards dusk. Their level of activity increases during the mating season, however, and lions may mate every fifteen minutes or so around the clock, when the female is receptive.

Many species only come together briefly to mate, as is the case with ocelots (*Felis pardalis*) shown here.

remaining there at night, although this depends to some extent on species. Generally, it is the larger cats which stray further afield: female leopards, for example, sometimes leave their offspring alone for as long as seventy-two hours at a time.

The young cats develop quite rapidly, and although at first their movements are restricted, they are able to crawl quite adequately over short distances. This enables them to find their littermates, which provides the basis for thermo-regulatory behaviour – by snuggling together the young cats can conserve their body heat, but if they become too warm they move away from each other so there is no longer direct contact between them. If disturbed a kitten is likely to defend itself by hissing loudly, and possibly attempting to scratch, even before its eyes have opened. This normally occurs between one and two weeks of age, although there is quite wide variation within this period.

Generally, the eyes of the larger species open much earlier – indeed, lion cubs can often see from birth. This may be related to their degree of exposure – smaller cats give birth in places where their offspring are better concealed. Tigers provide support for this theory as well, since there appear to be marked variations between subspecies. Bengal tigers may be born with their eyes open, whereas in the Siberian race this may not occur until the young are about two and a half weeks old.

DEVELOPMENT OF THE YOUNG CATS

As they grow older, play assumes a growing significance in the lives of the young cats. Their co-ordination improves, so they can begin to acquire skills essential to their subsequent survival as well as socialize with their littermates. There is no obvious dominance: one cat may play a dominant role in pursuing another, and then the roles may be reversed.

There is also no obvious attempt to inflict injuries on their fellows, although ritualized fighting is a frequent component of play. Clear differences may be observed in these games, depending upon the species. Cheetahs, for example, use their paws to knock each other over; they will use the same technique later in life to overcome their quarry at speed. If the mother has only a single offspring, she adopts a more playful role, apparently to compensate for lack of siblings.

Hunting can be a very dangerous pastime, especially for the inexperienced, and success often depends on judging distance correctly and knowing exactly when to strike. These skills are developed through play. Encouraging the offspring to recognize and kill prey is a gradual process. It typically commences with the female bringing back an animal which she has killed, and eating it in front of the young cats. Then, at a later stage, she will encourage them to eat. Further refinement occurs when the mother starts to bring back live but often immobilized prey, to enable the youngsters to practise their killing technique. This usually starts when they are rising three months old.

Initially, kittens may be reluctant to strike, but competitiveness within the litter usually encourages one of the group to inflict a fatal blow. This seems to be a key period in their development. If a young cat has no opportunity to make a kill at this stage, it may have difficulty in acquiring the skill later in life. Such problems were encountered in Africa by Joy and George Adamson with both a lioness and a cheetah, and a similar situation frequently arises in domestic cats.

Young cats, such as this snow leopard (*Panthera uncia*), start to accumulate their hunting skills through play, and by learning from their mother. Even so, starvation remains a real threat in their early days of independence.

While there are few creatures which will prey on the large adult cats, their offspring are vulnerable to predation, and may even be killed by a male seeking to mate with their mother. A young snow leopard (*Panthera uncia*) is shown here.

Those reared in farm surroundings prove to be far more competent hunters in later life than, at the other extreme, pure-bred cats reared in the relative isolation of a cattery. In this respect, lion cubs, which live in a group, are at an advantage over other cats, as they will have a greater opportunity to watch hunting behaviour.

Female cheetahs have been observed releasing a Thomson's gazelle for their cubs to overcome, and tigers too have been recorded bringing down quarry which is left for their offspring to kill without parental assistance. Only if the unfortunate creature tries to escape will the female intervene, restraining it within reach of her cubs. It appears that the young instinctively know how to kill – they are not shown how to do so by their mother.

Subsequently she will start to take then on hunting trips with her, although her offspring's inexperience reduces her success rate. On these occasions game frequently escapes before the adult cat has reached a point from which she can hope to make a successful strike.

Young cats stay in close contact with their mother from the time that they leave the den permanently, at around six weeks of age, to the break-up of the family, which can occur up to two years later. The youngsters are capable of communicating with her in the ultra-sonic range, while their mother will growl if she senses danger. They then 'freeze', and remain hidden until she signals that it is safe for them to re-emerge and join her.

Lion cubs tend to have a longer developmental period than other cats, perhaps because there is less pressure on them to hunt to obtain food. They are generally allowed to scavenge on the kills made by other members of the pride, and are tolerated even by the dominant male. A young lion is unlikely to make its first independent kill before the age of fifteen months, and possibly much older.

Overall, the bigger cats remain dependent on their mother for longer than their smaller relatives. This may be linked to the relative dangers involved in making a kill. Whereas smaller cats tend to prey on animals smaller than themselves, the bigger species not only have to master the ability to catch their quarry, but must also learn to overcome an animal which is quite capable of inflicting serious if not fatal injuries on them. Even a blow from a zebra's hooves can be deadly. A prolonged period of exposure to their mother's hunting techniques should enable them to learn by example.

Another relevant factor to the break-up of cat families is the arrival of the permanent teeth. A cat which has shed its milk teeth but has not yet regrown its canines will be at an acute disadvantage when it comes to killing prey, and must continue to wait for its independence.

The dispersal of young cats is not clearly understood, but it appears that females rarely venture as far afield as males, often establishing a territory close to that of their mother. Lionesses may remain with the pride, but males will invariably be driven out.

HAZARDS AND MORTALITY

This is influenced by various factors, including the availability of prey and hunting pressures, especially those imposed by humans, which can have a devastating impact in some areas. One study involving Canadian lynx found that the annual mortality rate was around 90 per cent, with trapping accounting for 80 per cent

When times are hard, bobcats (*Lynx rufus*) will widen their choice of prey, feeding on a much greater variety of species.

of this figure. Young lynxes were particularly vulnerable to being trapped, with over three-quarters of all offspring being killed within their first year.

This species is also affected by the availability of its main prey, the snowshoe hare. Researchers have discovered that lynx numbers increase significantly in a cyclical fashion and then decline over a period of 9.6 years. When prey is plentiful the young lynxes have a higher rate of survival, and average litter size is larger. Then, as the availability of these hares declines, the adult lynx produce fewer offspring and the young females may not breed at all, until the numbers of hares begin to increase again.

Other cats can respond to temporary shortages because they are able to prey upon a wider range of species. Bobcats in Florida, for example, take mainly cottontail rabbits and cotton rats when these animals are plentiful. But in years when a population crash occurs they will switch to other prey, and may then treble the number of species which they take – up to twenty-one in total, according to one study.

Some species of cat appear less able to adapt to prey shortages than others: leopards, for instance, often fare badly when food is hard to find. Young cubs in particular are at risk from starvation. Cheetahs are also especially vulnerable if they are unable to obtain prey through injury.

Predation poses a threat to cat populations, and human persecution is a constant hazard. Wolves, hyenas and jackals represent a danger, especially for cubs and smaller wild cats. Leopards will prey on cheetahs, and cannibalism, although rare, is not unknown, particularly in the case of lions. Attacks from buffaloes are a major cause of mortality in young lionesses in the Serengeti National Park, although disease is probably one of the major killers of lions in this region.

As with domestic cats, there are a number of viruses to which wild cats are susceptible. These include the typical components of so-called 'cat flu', as well as feline panleucopaenia, both of which can result in high mortality in susceptible populations, although there is evidence of natural resistance in some New World species. Not all viruses are necessarily harmful, however. Based on blood sampling studies, over 90 per cent of the lions in the Kruger National Park are now positive for the Feline Immunodeficiency Virus (FIV), and this figure has increased by just under a third since the mid-1970s. Yet there is no obvious sign of illness in these lions, and the population is growing.

Leopards are sufficiently large and powerful to kill cheetahs. Although they cannot outpace them, they will use guile to ambush them, with youngsters being particularly vulnerable.

Once they have gained maturity, most large cats live out their natural life span, which can be as much as twenty years for lions like this Asian female (*Panthera leo*), although they are vulnerable to injury and human persecution.

Wild cats usually suffer from parasites, ranging from intestinal worms to blood parasites, lice, mites and ticks, but they do not often cause serious disease. The number of parasites typically increases when the cat is in poor health or suffering from malnutrition. This state may encourage the development of tuberculosis, a chronic bacterial disease which is ultimately likely to prove fatal.

In spite of all the hazards faced by wild cats, there is evidence that once they are mature, and assuming that prey is readily obtainable and they are not subjected to excessive human persecution, then they will achieve their natural life-span. This is probably between ten and fifteen years in the case of the smaller species, and perhaps twenty years or so for lions and tigers. Even in the Serengeti, where prey is highly migratory and periods of relative starvation are likely, about one in ten lions manages to attain old age and may then be cared for by other pride members, which allow it to feed at their kills. Other solitary cats are less fortunate and may face a slow death from starvation once they cannot hunt or find food to scavenge.

Chapter 4
Evolution and Distribution

EARLIEST ANCESTORS

The origins of predatory, flesh-eating mammals date back to the late Cretaceous period, about 65 million years ago. The earliest members of this group are thought to have evolved from insectivorous ancestors, and with the extinction of the dinosaurs they became increasingly dominant on the planet.

Initially, the creodonts were the most significant of these creatures: their earliest known remains are fossils from the early years of the Tertiary period, which followed the Cretaceous. Over fifty different genera are known, divided into two families known as Hyaenodontidae and Oxyaenidae. Their remains have been found around the world, except in South America and Australia.

The oxyaenids tended to be relatively small and were characterized by short, stocky limbs and long tails. About a dozen forms are at present recognized, discernible from their hyaenodontid relatives by their teeth. In the oxyaenids the first upper molar and the second lower molar on each side work together to form the carnassial or shearing teeth, whereas in the hyaenodontids this function is performed by the second upper molar and the third lower molar.

Several oxyaenids which inhabited what is now North America and Eurasia did achieve a large size. The biggest form recorded to date is *Sarkastodon*, which lived during the late Eocene epoch, around 35 million years ago, and was somewhat larger than a bear. It inhabited the plains of Central Asia, where there were correspondingly bulky ungulates such as the grontotheres and early rhinoceroses. *Sarkastodon* grew to at least 3 m (10 ft) long, and evolved massive teeth to prey upon such animals. As a stocky and relatively slow hunter, however, it may have scavenged for food as well, rather like modern bears.

Other, smaller creodonts were more athletic in appearance. Within the hyaenodont group, the *Hyaenodon* genus itself evolved quite late during the history of the creodonts. Its period of dominance extended from 60 million to 30 million years ago, before it finally disappeared in the late Miocene epoch, just 7 million years ago.

The remains of *Hyaenodon* are widespread, having been discovered in Europe, Asia, Africa and North America. Individual species ranged in size from that of a stoat up to that of a hyaena. These mammals had long, slim legs and walked on their toes in a digitigrade manner, rather than using the soles of their feet like the oxyaenids. They would therefore have been able to run quite effectively after prey, although not with the pace of today's felines. It is likely that they too scavenged as well as hunted. Some other hyaenodontids appear to have been more specialized in their feeding habits; *Quercytherium*, whose remains have been uncovered in France, is an example. Its broad premolars suggest that it may have fed on molluscs, crushing their shells in its mouth. An indicator of later developments on the evolutionary pathway was the appearance of sabre-toothed hyaenodontids during the later part of the Eocene epoch in North America, although they do not appear to have been particularly common.

All the creodonts possessed claws, and within their mouths was a formidable array of forty-four teeth. These show clear signs of specialization, with a canine present in each jaw, along with three incisors, four pre-molars and three molars. Carnassial teeth can also be distinguished, but they differ from those in true carnivores, where they comprise the fourth pre-molar in the upper jaw and the first lower molar. Evidence of this particular pattern of dentition is first seen in a small group of mammals called the miacids, which appeared during the Paleocene epoch, around 60 million years ago.

The origins of this family are unclear, but they may have been an early offshoot from the creodonts. The oldest miacids are known from discoveries made in North America and Europe. A typical example was *Miacis* itself, which lived in the region of present-day Germany. Its remains indicate that *Miacis* was probably not unlike a pine marten (*Martes martes*) in appearance. Measuring about 20 cm (8 in) in length, *Miacis* had flexible forelimbs, suggesting that it was an agile climber equally at home in the trees and on the ground. It is likely to have been an opportunistic predator, catching birds and small mammals as well as eating insects and possibly fruit. Unlike later carnivores, *Miacis* retained a full complement of forty-four teeth.

FORERUNNERS OF TODAY'S CATS

By the time that the Eocene epoch drew to a close the majority of creodonts had become extinct, for reasons which are not clearly understood. It has been suggested that the rise of the miacids was achieved because their brain capacity evolved faster than that of the creodonts. Overall, however, there was no significant variation in brain capacity between the two groups – the only evident difference was expansion of separate areas of the neocortex which probably had no functional significance.

The miacids themselves were a diverse group of mammals, and it may simply have been that they were more adaptable. In any event, the forerunners of contemporary carnivores were already emerging by the end of the Eocene. One group was to give rise to dogs, bears, seals, badgers, weasels and other related mammals. Yet it was the lineage which led to the aeluroids that ultimately evolved into today's cats. The ancestors of all felids are thought to have split off from civet stock. Evidence for this relationship has been unearthed in the Quercy phosphorite deposits of France, where the remains of *Proailurus* have been found. This was a relatively small animal, with a noticeably long tail and quite long legs. It used to be classified as a civet, but is now believed to be an ancestral felid.

The evolutionary history of cats is not clear, partly because their ancestors tended to live in forested areas where their remains were not likely to be fossilized. Contemporary thinking now sees two distinct lines. The first stems from *Proailurus*, which was a forerunner of *Pseudaelurus*. The pattern of dentition of *Pseudaelurus* is not unlike that of a modern cat, while in terms of appearance it stood quite tall and had five toes on each foot.

Subsequent divisions of this lineage gave rise to a number of other genera including all the contemporary species, and various sabre-toothed forms which are now extinct. Best-known is *Smilodon*, a genus which existed during the late Pleistocene epoch, about eleven thousand years ago. Although sometimes known as sabre-toothed tigers, these felids are not related to tigers.

78

The sabre-tooths

Smilodon averaged about 1.2 m (4 ft) in length, and was unusual in that its tail was short. Its huge head was supported by the powerful muscles of its forequarters. The jaws themselves could open to an angle of 120°, which allowed the huge canines in the upper jaw to be driven downwards into prey with maximum impact.

These teeth were specially adapted to penetrate the thick skins of the bison and mammoths on which these cats preyed. In cross-section the teeth were oval, which enabled them to retain their strength while slicing through flesh with little resistance. Their dagger-like qualities were further enhanced by serrations along the front and back of each tooth.

The hunting method of *Smilodon* differed from that of contemporary felids, being inevitably more bloody. It literally hacked its prey to death, tearing through the skin with the aim of rupturing a major blood vessel which would result in a fatal haemorrhage, or of disembowelling the unfortunate animal. The enlarged canines preclude the possibility that *Smilodon* killed by slicing through the spinal cord, since these teeth would have been very vulnerable to injury by the vertebrae.

Smilodon is well known through the remains which were unearthed from 1913 at a former tar pit at Rancho La Brea, now part of downtown Los Angeles. This major find, now housed in the George C. Page Museum of La Brea Discoveries in Los Angeles, enabled over a million fossilized bones of mammals to be excavated over a period of nearly twenty years. Nearly 10 per cent of the remains are of *Smilodon fatalis*, which was similar in size to an African lion, and these fossil finds

Since the ancestors of today's cats apparently occurred in forested areas relatively little has been discovered about them in terms of fossilized remains. In turn, their revolutionary pathway is not well understood. This is an Asian example of the wild cat (*Felis lybica*).

are thought to represent up to two thousand sabre-toothed cats which perished here. Such a discovery helps to provide a clear insight into the lifestyles of these fearsome predators.

It is thought that they became trapped over many years while pursuing prey, or may have been attracted by early horses or other animals already enmeshed in the tar pit, and ultimately died here themselves.

In addition to its teeth, *Smilodon* had powerful claws, which would have enabled it to grasp on to prey. Yet they have a very different arrangement from those of all modern cats. Instead of the largest claw being in the centre of each paw it is on the innermost digit, with a progressive reduction in size across the other toes. The significance is not known, but this positioning of the claws may have helped to provide secure anchorage points when attacking prey. The claws could be retracted when the cats were resting.

Certainly, *Smilodon* was not equipped for a long chase. It lacked a long tail, which provides balance during a hunt, and presumably relied instead on surprising its quarry. The front legs were especially powerful, and doubtless were used in combination with the teeth to inflict the fatal blows.

The remains uncovered in Rancho La Brea suggest that these cats formed social communities. Some of the fossils reveal very severe injuries; although they subsequently healed, it is doubtful whether the cat could have hunted in the interim. While scavenging could have offered a possible means of survival, it is more likely that other sabre-tooths allowed an injured individual to feed unmolested on their kill.

Hunting in the usual *Smilodon* fashion was clearly a hazardous pursuit, even under normal circumstances. Virtually all the bones found at the Rancho La Brea site show signs of trauma or disease. Excessive joint movements resulted in osteoarthritis, with fusion of the spinal column also apparent in some cases. There is little doubt that *Smilodon* relied upon a highly aggressive hunting technique, launching itself with considerable force at its prey. This is reflected in the compression injuries evident along the vertebral column in many instances, with the initial impact taking place on the chest and then reverberating through the body. Nor were the teeth immune from injury. They could be broken or lost, and this would undoubtedly have handicapped their hunting abilities severely – the cats would have had great difficulty in penetrating the hide of their large and relatively dangerous prey before it could be killed.

It is tempting to suppose that *Smilodon* was a social cat, with a lifestyle not dissimilar from that of today's lions. Living in groups, they may also have hunted collectively. The landscape of the Rancho La Brea at this time consisted of plains with sparse tree cover, where the sabre-tooths would have ambushed unsuspecting herbivores as they browsed. Fighting between rival males for dominance could have accounted for a high proportion of the bite injuries, typically on the shoulders and back seen in the fossilized remains.

While *Smilodon* is undoubtedly the best known of the sabre-toothed cats, a number of other forms are recognized. *Megantereon* resembled *Smilodon* in appearance, apart from its so-called dirk teeth (from the Scottish word for a dagger), which were long and relatively thin – not truly reminiscent of a sabre. The earliest remains of *Megantereon* were discovered in northern India and date back to the late Miocene epoch, some 7 million years ago. It established itself in the Mediterranean area and reached southern Africa, as well as North America, before dying out in the early Pleistocene. It is thought that *Megantereon* had a similar lifestyle to *Smilodon*, but was probably more solitary by nature.

Another group of cats in the sabre-toothed category also differed in the shape and length of these teeth. These cats are referred to as scimitar-toothed, and had shorter, flatter canines that curled backwards in the shape of a scimitar. *Homotherium* is one of the best-known examples of this group, which apparently had a wide distribution: *Homotherium* remains have been found in parts of Europe, Asia and Africa, as well as North America. It lived during the Pleistocene epoch, dying out at about the end of the last Ice Age some fourteen thousand years ago. Its extinction may have been linked to the decline of its prey, which appears to have been mammoths. Remains of both creatures have been discovered close to each other.

In appearance *Homotherium* had a sloping profile, with its forequarters higher than its hindquarters. Another unusual feature was its method of walking. This was plantigrade, meaning that the animal placed its entire foot on the ground as it moved, rather than just its toes which is a characteristic feature of most cats. *Homotherium* did, however, possess retractile claws, enabling it to strike more effectively – a feature also evident in *Smilodon*.

Controversy has persisted over the hunting techniques of *Homotherium* and other sabre-toothed cats. Yet there is no doubt that their type and arrangement of teeth places certain restraints on the skull structure and overlying musculature. This is clear from a comparison of these felids with other sabre-toothed mammals. While the evolution of greatly elongated canines was first recorded in creodonts, it is also found in early marsupials. This totally unrelated group of mammals, distinguished by the abdominal pouch in which the young develop after being born in an immature state, evolved during the late Cretaceous period, between 100 and 75 million years ago.

It was only in the late Miocene epoch, however, some 7 million years ago, that the thylacosmilids – large marsupial predators – evolved. *Thylacosmilus* itself grew to about 1.2 m (4 ft) in length, and lived in what is now South America. The canine teeth in its upper jaw came down well below the level of the lower ones, and continued growing throughout the animal's life. This does not appear to have been the case with sabre-toothed cats, which, unlike *Thylacosmilus*, also retained their incisor teeth. But in both instances it is the musculature of the head, rather than the jaw muscles, that provides the thrust for the teeth.

It was also necessary for the mouth to have a wider gape, and this resulted in the adjustment of the temporalis muscle. In turn, the coronoid process on the skull was reduced in size, which led to suggestions that neither of these two groups of mammals could exert much force with their carnassial teeth. But since their teeth were located further back in the mouth, it was possible for them to exert greater pressure.

The elongated canines were relatively fragile, however, and liable to shear unless plunged directly into the prey. Care also had to be taken to avoid contact with bone, which could also have severely damaged the teeth. This argument provides further evidence to suggest that sabre-toothed cats did not kill their prey in a 'conventional' felid manner, by striking at the neck. They relied instead on a quick strike, catching their larger prey unawares and inflicting a fatal wound before withdrawing and waiting until the unfortunate animal collapsed. Yet more evidence to support this theory is supplied by the jaw musculature.

Sabre-toothed cats were not able to cling on to prey with their jaws, which were relatively weak.

The reasons for the decline and ultimate extinction of the sabre-tooths are unclear. There may have been a decline in their slow-moving prey, as in the case of *Homotherium*. The cats' relative lack of pace would then have proved a distinct disadvantage, with the increasing availability of smaller, faster and more nimble creatures such as rats and mice during the Pleistocene epoch which they would have been ill-equipped to catch.

Overall, it was the lack of adaptability in hunting techniques which was probably the major reason why sabre-toothed cats died out – although hunting pressure by early humans may have played a part as well. Certainly, the fact that four distinct lines of mammals with enlarged canines in their upper jaw evolved and then died out does suggest that this pattern of dentition was too specialized.

PROBLEMS OF EVOLUTION AND CLASSIFICATION

Unfortunately, the evolution of the felids remains controversial. The traditional view divided the ancestral forms into two categories, which started with the paleofelids, the group of cats known as the false sabre-tooths, and which included *Nimravus*. The neofelids or 'true cats' followed later, during the Miocene epoch which began some 25 million years ago; other sabre-tooths such as *Smilodon* are grouped here. The relative dates of these evolutionary pathways suggested that the paleofelids may have been the ancestors of the neofelids. Yet comparison of the sabre-toothed forms shows highly distinctive differences between the paleofelids and the neofelids, which implies that they were actually unrelated groups. This view is based on the anatomy of the ear and other skull features, such as the coronoid process which is most prominent in the neofelids.

It is now accepted that linking the two groups in this simplistic fashion is incorrect, but devising an alternative evolutionary pathway has proved just as problematical because of gaps in the fossil record. It is impossible for people today to understand the pressures which shaped the evolutionary processes of cats back in history. The lack of complete skeletons makes it very difficult to establish a composite picture of members of the genera involved, and of course there is always the distinct likelihood that other remains await discovery. So the factual basis for a particular theory can be sketchy. One such proposal which suggests that the nimravids split from the aeluroid lineage at an early stage in their history is based on a perceived similarity between the aeluroid bulla and a single piece of bone from a nimravid. This shows just how little evidence may be available upon which to base a hypothesis.

Interpretation relies to a great extent on determining the relative importance of the 'uniqueness' of features. For example, the fact that some members of both the Nimravidae and Felidae families had elongated upper canines suggests they are related – yet not all genera in the groups had this style of dentition, and it is known to have evolved in other, unrelated groups such as the marsupials. This tends to lessen its significance when defining the relationship between these families.

Similar criticism can be made of the theory which links the nimravids to the arctoids, essentially on the basis of their carnassial tooth patterns. What is clear, however, is that the ancestral form of both paleofelids and the neofelids did not

Early relatives of leopard cats (*Felis bengalensis*) lived in Asia a million years ago.

have enlarged canines, and that this feature arose as a later stage of evolution.

For classification purposes palaeontologists have focused on the auditory bulla, which encases the middle ear. In the miacids there was no ossification (bony structure) here, extending beyond the ring which supports the tympanic membrane. Early carnivores either lacked ossification altogether or had a very restricted amount of bony tissue here. This applied also to the nimravids, with the notable exception of the most recent example of the family, christened *Barbourofelis*, which lived in North America until 7 million years ago. In contrast the aeluroid group, encompassing cats and civets, is characterized by a very distinctive ossification of the auditory bulla.

It has even been suggested that the nimravids were more closely related to contemporary canids – ancestors of today's dogs – than to felids. According to this school of thought, the fact that the nimravids evolved elongated canines was simply coincidental, in the same way that *Thylacosmilus* developed this type of dentition. Support for this argument is provided by *Thylacoleo*, sometimes known as the marsupial 'lion'. Remains of *Thylacoleo*, dating from the Miocene to the Pleistocene, have been unearthed in Australia. It developed elongated incisors, rather than canine teeth, which could have been used for stabbing prey. In overall appearance *Thylacoleo* was almost certainly not dissimilar to a felid, and yet represented a totally separate group. It preyed on wombats and large marsupial herbivores.

MODERN CATS

Contemporary felids are believed to have stemmed from the *Pseudaelurus* lineage, which appeared some 20 million years ago. Unfortunately the fossil evidence, particularly of smaller species, is limited, mainly because of their distribution. They inhabited forested areas, where suitable conditions for fossilization were less likely than in relatively open ground.

The oldest remains so far discovered of the likely ancestor of the European wild cat, christened Martelli's wild cat (*Felis silvestris lunensis*), date from the Early Pleistocene, about two million years ago. It may have existed through to the Mid-Pleistocene before being replaced by its modern form.

Some felids had a wider distribution in the past: Pallas's cat, for instance, extended its range into Europe during the last Ice Age whereas today it is confined to parts of Asia. Jungle cats may also have lived in Europe. In Asia, remains of small leopard cats dating back to the early part of the Middle Pleistocene period (about one million years ago) have been unearthed on the Sunda Islands of Indonesia; they have also been found in Neolithic remains on Java.

The fossil record for this genus is equally sketchy in the Americas. One of the earliest finds is from the Late Pliocene, about 3 million years ago, and suggests that this cat, christened *Felis vorohuensis*, was probably an ancestral form of today's pampas cat which still occurs here in Argentina. An early form of the

The lynx appears to have evolved in the Old World, and then crossed from Asia into North America before sea levels rose around 15,000 years ago, severing the connection between the continents.

ocelot was established in Florida around 100,000 years ago, right at the end of the Pleistocene period, and *Felis wiedii amnicola*, the ancestor of today's margay, could be found in North America at the same time. Both the margay itself and the jaguarundi also appear to have evolved at around the same time – very recently in geological terms.

The evolution of the lynx is better documented in the fossil record; it first appeared in Africa, during the Late Pliocene between 3 and 4 million years ago. This species has been christened the Issoire Lynx (*Lynx issidorensis*). Taller in stature than the contemporary lynx, in overall appearance it was more like members of the genus *Felis*. This species became widely distributed: its remains have also been unearthed in Europe, where it has been claimed to be the ancestral form of the Spanish or pardel lynx, which is sometimes recognized as a separate species, *Lynx pardinus*. In Asia its remains have been found in China, where it gave rise to the Eurasian lynx (*Lynx lynx*), which spread into Europe about 100,000 years ago. To the east, the Issoire lynx moved into North America via the Bering land bridge (now the Bering Straits) which linked Asia and North America at this stage. Here it evolved into the bobcat (*Lynx rufus*), while the Eurasian lynx developed here into the North America lynx (*Lynx canadensis*).

The various forms of the lynx were in conflict with other felids, however, notably leopards in Eurasia and pumas in North America. This factor was probably responsible for a decline in their size, enabling them to establish a separate niche rather than having to compete directly with these established species.

The earliest forms of the puma appeared about 3 million years ago in North America. At this stage they too were larger, and more suited than the contemporary puma to pursuing prey on the ground.

The jungle cat (*Felis chaus*) shows a considerable variation in size throughout its range. Those from India are smaller than those occurring further north.

The ancestor of today's leopards originated about 2 million years ago, in the Indian region. From here they spread eastwards and southwards across Asia, and different forms evolved. Those found on Java were much larger than the Chinese races. The remains of leopards have also been unearthed in Europe, where similar disparities in size occurred. The earliest recorded remains of European leopards are approximately $2\frac{1}{2}$ million years old; as the glaciers moved back and forth across the continent, so the various populations became isolated and evolved on separate lines.

There was a close relationship between these early leopards and jaguars. Although now confined to South America, jaguars actually evolved in Eurasia and pushed southwards from here into Africa. Leopards were also found here, being established at the southern end of the continent by the Early Pleistocene.

Jaguars reached North America, crossing from Asia via the Bering land bridge about 3 million years ago. At this stage they were bigger and better suited to running than present-day jaguars, but as the land became more forested so their build modified to become more suited to climbing. By the Mid-Pleistocene they had reached the area that is now Bolivia, and a giant form had evolved in present-day Argentina by the latter part of this epoch.

Cheetahs also used to be found over a bigger area than their present range suggests. The ancestral form, *Acinonyx pardinensis,* was significantly larger than today's species, being about the size of a lion. However, in virtually all other

Leopards (*Panthera pardus*) may have lived in Europe over two million years ago.

aspects, aside from slight variations in the skull and teeth, it was unmistakably similar to the cheetah itself, which had evolved by the Late Pleistocene. It is believed that cheetahs may also have existed for a period in North America, as two likely species have been identified here. The oldest, christened *Acinonyx studeri*, existed $2\frac{1}{2}$ million years ago, while the other, known as *Acinonyx trumani*, lived on the North American continent as recently as twelve thousand years ago, preying on deer.

The origins of lions can be traced back to Africa, and although there is some debate over the authenticity of the remains, the earliest evidence of their existence here dates back between 700,000 and 500,000 years. The precise relationships between the early lions and other *Panthera* species are unclear, however, even after lions had moved northwards into Eurasia about 250,000 years ago. Here the remains of the Tuscany lion, which lived in the forests of northern Italy, have been found. Although equivalent in size to a small lion, these cats had a different dentition and could have been more closely related to leopards.

Climatic changes during the Middle Pleistocene saw a reduction in the range of the ancestral form of the lion, and the emergence of distinctive species. The cave lion (*Panthera spelaea*) was probably similar in appearance to today's lions, with its distribution centred on Europe. Human hunting pressures may have played a part in its decline, with the last cave lions occurring in the vicinity of the Balkans.

Lions also expanded their range into the Americas for a period. The American lion (*Panthera atrox*) is believed to have evolved in Asia, however, crossing via the Bering land bridge into the western part of North America. From here lions spread southwards, reaching as far as modern-day Peru by the end of the Pleistocene. Then climatic changes occurred, which affected their pattern of distribution. The growth of forests, with a corresponding reduction in open plains, meant that lions gradually died out in the New World, and other species such as jaguars became dominant.

Tigers, which evolved in eastern Asia during the Late Pliocene, have always had a more limited range than lions. A smaller, ancestral form of today's species lived in China, and about 2 million years ago tigers were already well distributed into south-eastern Asia. Some were much bigger than those seen today: particularly large forms are known to have occurred during the Late Pleistocene both in China and on the island of Java. A notable variance in size is also evident in tiger populations today in different parts of their range, which has since contracted. Tigers no longer occur in Japan, where they died out less than a million years ago; their most marked decline, however, has probably taken place over the course of the past century, largely because of human persecution.

Distinctions between the various subspecies of tiger can be made on anatomical grounds. The Chinese tiger (*Panthera tigris amoyensis*), with its eye sockets positioned well forwards and a short cranium, is regarded as the oldest surviving form, providing further evidence that the species arose in this area. From here, tigers are believed to have invaded south-eastern Asia and ultimately India, while a second expansion saw their distribution extend westwards to the vicinity of the Caspian Sea and beyond.

Fossilized evidence of the other large cats found in Asia is less well known. Snow leopards could have arisen in northern China during the Mid-Pleistocene, before spreading westwards into Asia. Remains of early forms of the clouded leopard have been unearthed in Java, and although this species subsequently died out there, it still occurs on the neighbouring island of Sumatra and in other parts of south-east Asia, where it has been present for possibly 2 million years.

UNRAVELLING THE PAST IN THE LABORATORY

The lack of knowledge about the ancestry of cats has also handicapped current taxonomy. Without a proper understanding of their historical relationships it is difficult to establish a meaningful systematic approach to the scientific classification of today's cats.

During recent years, however, the application of laboratory techniques, rather than exclusive reliance on the fossil record, has provided a new insight into the evolutionary process that gave rise to contemporary cats. Early investigations of this type centred on chromosomal maps, known as karyotypes, which enable the number and structure of the chromosomes containing the genetic material to be studied. This work suggested that there was a clear division between the Old World and New World cats, with those presumably stemming from the Old World, including the jaguar, jaguarundi and puma, having an additional pair of chromosomes, making nineteen in total. Subsequent refinement of this technique included a comparison of the structure of the bacula in different species. This bone, present in the penis, is used to distinguish between numerous species of carnivore.

The cheetah's ancestors ranged more widely than the modern form, and may even have occurred in North America.

Domestication of the cat, from African wild cat stock, began over 9,000 years ago.

Unfortunately, this approach did not resolve the controversy over classification, because it led to the proposal that eighteen separate genera should be recognized – far more than is generally accepted. It also gave rise to the suggestion that the jaguarundi in North America, together with the wild cat and other species from Europe and Asia, trace their ancestry back to members of the subgenus *Prionailurus*, which embraces the rusty-spotted cat, the fishing cat, the flat-headed cat and the leopard cat.

New work is now focusing not on chromosomes, but rather on the genetic material itself – DNA – to track the history of the felids. The strands of deoxyribose nucleic acid (DNA) are arranged in the form of a double helix, within which there are different sequences of acids and bases. By comparing the structure of DNA from related species it is possible to assess how far they have diverged from each other, and when the split is likely to have occurred.

The conclusion drawn was that the major evolutionary development which ultimately resulted in today's species occurred about 12 million years ago. This led to the cats now present in South America, and, about 2 million years later, to a separate lineage which were the ancestors of today's Old World species. More

89

recently, between 4 and 6 million years ago, the Old World stock gave rise to the pantherine lineage, which is now represented by the puma, serval and jaguarundi.

The most revolutionary aspect of this work concerned the cheetah, which has always been rather a feline anomaly on grounds of its appearance. This gave rise to the long-standing belief that it had evolved in isolation, having split off from the feline lineage at an early stage. In fact the genetic evidence makes it a member of the pantherine group.

More recent work has confirmed these findings, and suggested that the clouded leopard was the original species to split off, around 7 million years ago. The snow leopard followed, approximately 3 million years later, with the other big cats dividing off from the lynxes just 2 million years ago.

This approach has cut across the previous systems of classification. Evidence for its accuracy is provided by comparing our existing knowledge of the evolution of species, based on their fossil records, and the comparative timespan obtained from laboratory studies. It is likely that biochemical investigations of this type will provide further insight into feline evolution over the years ahead.

Chapter 5
The Feline Family

While taxonomists argue over the precise number of species in the family Felidae, it is generally agreed that they can be split into two main groups. The big cats such as the lion and tiger, the majority of which fall within the *Panthera* genus, constitute the subfamily Pantherinae. Smaller species comprising the genus *Felis*, with the notable exception of the marbled cat (*Pardofelis marmorata*), make up the subfamily Felinae.

Most taxonomic proposals list the cheetah separately at present, in spite of growing evidence that it should be included in the Pantherinae grouping. The recently discovered onza is also likely to be included in this category.

While initially the Tshushima cat was believed to be a new species in the genus *Felis*, it is now widely accepted that it is actually a subspecies of the leopard cat (*Felis bengalensis*). It appears to be most closely related to the Manchurian race (*Felis bengalensis manchurica*).

The classificatory system operates through a series of ranks which identify the cat down to an individual race or particular population. Taking the kodkod as an example:

Order	Mammalia
Family	Felidae
Subfamily	Felinae
Genus	*Felis*
Species	*Felis guigna*
Subspecies	*Felis guigna guigna*
	Felis guigna tigrillo

The so-called nominate subspecies, which is the first to have been described, can be identified by the repetition of the specific name. Here it is *Felis guigna guigna*. The listing of subspecies can be controversial, with zoologists disagreeing over their validity.

SUBFAMILY FELINAE

SMALL CATS OF THE OLD WORLD

European wild cat *Felis silvestris*

DISTRIBUTION
Extends westwards from the Caucasus, along the Mediterranean to the Atlantic. On its northern border it extends through Poland and Germany to France, and an isolated population is also present in Scotland, but it no longer occurs in Scandinavia.

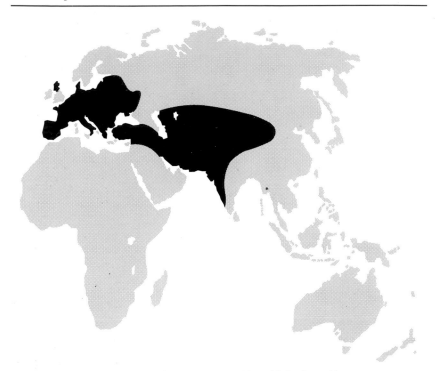

Distribution of the European wild cat (*Felis silvestris*).

Taxonomists disagree about the classification of the wild cat. Some recognize both a European and an African species, whereas others consider them synonymous and view them simply as subspecies.

In Scotland the European wild cat is no longer found south of a line drawn between Glasgow and Edinburgh; their last remaining stronghold is the northeast of the country. Even where conditions seem suitable wild cats are not numerous, and they are decidedly uncommon in western and north-western Scotland, according to a survey carried out between 1983 and 1987. This investigation led to wild cats being afforded full legal protection in 1988, when their killing was outlawed.

The Scottish form of the European wild cat is relatively dark, with distinctive tabby striping. It is stockily built, but has a broader head than domestic cats as well as a shorter tail with a blunt tip.

Remains of wild cats dating back over 2 million years have been unearthed in various parts of Britain, and they were common up until the end of the fifteenth century. Although the species has never been recorded from Ireland, it used to be widely distributed over England, Wales and Scotland. The skins of these cats were valued for clothing, while their dung, dried and made into a powder with bear's grease, mustard seed and other ingredients, was reputed to have offered an early cure for baldness!

Habitat change, coupled with hunting pressure, is thought to have led to the decline of the wild cat population throughout Britain. Clearance of woodland, which provides ideal habitat for these cats, had a serious detrimental impact on their numbers. While it is difficult to establish a comprehensive picture, records suggest that they were extinct in Northamptonshire by 1712, and had almost totally disappeared from Wales by 1826, before finally vanishing from this region in 1864. Wildcats were heavily persecuted as vermin, particularly by game-keepers, and by the 1850s had been exterminated south of the River Trent. The First World War gave these cats an opportunity to flourish in the temporary absence of harassment, and subsequently there has been a gradual reassessment of the threat posed by European wild cat populations to gamebirds and farmstock.

They may take red grouse in some areas, but this does not make much impact on grouse numbers, and similarly, reports of lamb killing are now considered to be highly exaggerated. These incidents can often be traced to a single individual, and removal of this cat usually prevents any recurrence. There is also a positive benefit in having wild cats in an area, because they help to control the numbers of rabbits, hares and rodents which may otherwise damage crops.

Unfortunately, the initial boom in numbers which accompanied the reduced level of persecution during the First World War has not been maintained. Records suggest that during the mid-1980s several hundred were being killed annually, notably on estates where grouse and pheasant shooting was a major source of income.

But a more recent and serious threat to the survival of the Scottish wild cat is hybridization with domestic cats. Britain's cat population has grown signifi-cantly in recent decades, rising from an estimated $3\frac{1}{2}$ million in 1971 to a figure approaching 7 million today. This means that wild cats are increasingly likely to come into contact with domestic or feral cats, and there is evidence that hybrid offspring are already widespread. It has even been suggested that the apparent slight increase in the wild cat population of Scotland over the past forty years has been largely the result of such hybridization, rather than reflecting a genuine increase in the numbers of wild cats.

Remote areas in the north and west of Scotland offer the greatest likelihood of finding pure wild cats. These regions have been consistently populated by them, and domestic cats are not numerous there. Yet these also tend to be the areas where persecution has been intensive, to the extent that nearly a third of all wild cat populations have suffered a decline in numbers, with only 8 per cent showing an increase, based on the recent surveys in Scotland.

But the adaptability of the wild cat does give hope for its future in Scotland, especially now that it has legal protection. Their diet depends very much on the countryside where they live. Studies undertaken in western Scotland reveal that rodents comprised up to half the diet here, while rabbits contributed less than 10 per cent. In contrast, in north-eastern Scotland over 90 per cent of their prey consisted of rabbits.

Their territorial area also varies greatly, as would be expected, depending on the availability of prey. The average territory is stated as being around 65 hec-tares (150 acres), but may be four times as large in open moorland. Males will cover considerable distances in search of a potential mate, whereas females appear to be more sedentary.

Seasonal fluctuation in weight is often apparent: males tend to be at their heaviest in winter. There is also a considerable variation in size. The largest on

In the European wild cat (*Felis silvestris*) markings in young cats are more distinctive than in adults. This species is similar in appearance to, but noticeably larger than, the domestic cat.

record had a total length, including its tail, of 117 cm (46 in); this animal was killed at Kinlockmoidart in Inverness-shire in October 1899. Although its weight was not recorded, adult European wild cats can range from about 3 kg to 7 kg ($6\frac{1}{2}$–$15\frac{1}{2}$ lb). There may well have been regional variations in size of the British wild cat when its distribution was more widespread. One record describes a cat obtained in Cumbria which was 1.5 m (60 in) in length, while other writers suggest that the average length may well have been 1.2 m (48 in).

The wild cat has established a fierce reputation in modern times; but in reality, like other cats, it will seek to avoid any encounter with people or dogs, only fighting as a last resort. Yet a mother with kittens is sufficiently ferocious to drive off a hungry and determined fox, and has even been known to seize a golden eagle which had taken one of her offspring.

If cornered, a wild cat tends to back off at first, seeking a solid rock or tree where it feels relatively secure. From this position, it will then act in a different manner from that of a domestic cat. Instead of arching its back and raising its tail, it crouches down, keeping the tail lowered, and rearing up on its forelimbs to emphasize its height. The ears are kept flattened against the head, while the teeth, particularly the long canines, are exposed. The cat maintains a constant menacing growl, spitting ferociously when its opponent moves. The aggression in this display is intended to startle, enabling the cat to escape without engaging in direct combat. This can take place at considerable speed.

In reality, however, wild cats face few predators in Scotland, since they are the only native cat found in this part of the world, and other, large carnivores such as wolves and bears are already extinct here. Only foxes and golden eagles may occasionally prey on these cats, usually taking kittens, but this appears to be rare.

The likelihood of seeing a wild cat within their limited area of distribution in Scotland is remote. Evidence of their presence, in the form of scats or footprints, is easier to find, but their dens are invariably well hidden. The best time to look for wild cats is during the autumn or early winter, when they may be hunting during the daytime. They may sometimes be seen basking in a sunny spot during the summer, but they are always very alert to any approach and will rapidly disappear if they sense the presence of an onlooker.

Much still remains to be learnt about the wild cat, with controversy surrounding even its reproductive potential. It has been suggested that they may breed more than once a year, but at least in Scotland, in the far north of their range, they probably have a more limited reproductive period. The female will begin to scent-mark more actively during February, and during this period starts calling to attract a mate. Mating typically occurs in March. The female then resumes her solitary lifestyle, and seeks out a den where she gives birth during May.

The typical litter comprises two to four youngsters, which are born with a full covering of fur. They are able to crawl within a couple of days, and from one week old are capable of spitting and responding aggressively if disturbed. Their eyes start to open between ten and thirteen days, and are bright blue at first, as with domestic cats. They then darken, and finally change to golden yellow when they are around five months old.

The male may bring food to the den, and so assist his mate in the rearing of their kittens. It appears that male wild cats are often monogamous, mating with the same female each year. Once she has kittens, however, the female may drive him away more forcibly if he attempts to approach too close, although there is at least one recorded sighting of a pair of wild cats out together with their kittens.

The kittens remain in the den until they are about a month old, by which time their mother is frequently off hunting for longer periods. They start playing in the vicinity of the den, and will be carried back there by their mother if they stray too far.

The weaning process has begun by the time that the kittens are about seven weeks old, and at this stage they are also starting to climb, albeit somewhat unsteadily. Their mother encourages them to develop their hunting skills, using her tail for this purpose. She waves it from side to side while resting and encourages the kittens to pounce on its black tip.

By two months old, the young wild cats are strong enough to accompany her further afield, and follow her example as she shows them how to catch craneflies, leaves and other similar items. Later she introduces them to real prey. By five months old they are fully independent and the family starts to break up, with the young females often departing first.

This breeding cycle ensures that kittens are born at the most favourable time of the year, when prey is likely to be plentiful. During the late summer they can then learn hunting skills which will enable them to sustain themselves over the winter ahead.

The habits of the European wild cat vary through its range. In Scotland, where tree cover in some areas is sparse, they may use rocky outcrops as dens, especially in the more mountainous areas. Coniferous forests are the favoured habitat of the species in Germany, while broad-leaved forests are preferred in the Caucasian area.

Small rodents appear to predominate in the wild cat's diet, although the actual prey varies according to region and season. In France, for example, the edible dormouse (*Glis glis*) is an important prey species in the autumn, while elsewhere voles and mice may comprise nearly all of the diet.

In mainland Europe, these cats have a similar history of persecution and habitat degradation to that of the Scottish wild cat. In addition, in some areas they face a major predator in the form of the Eurasian lynx – these cats will readily prey on their smaller relatives.

Differences between the various races are not as clear-cut on the basis of coat markings as might be anticipated. However, as a general guide, wild cats occurring in Asia are paler in coloration than those found further west.

KELLAS CAT

Recent attention in Scotland has focused on the case of the so-called Kellas cat, and the possible relationship of these black felines to the Scottish wild cat. While it is tempting to suggest that the Kellas cat is a new phenomenon, descriptions in Scottish folklore of very similar cats, known as the *cait sith*, meaning 'fairy cat', have been uncovered by Dr Karl Shuker. This creature is recorded as being relatively large, with an area of white fur on the throat, while the rest of its coat is said to have been glossy black.

The idea that the Kellas cat was not mere folklore, however, began in September 1984, when the *Forres Gazette*, published in Moray, gave details of a predominantly black cat which had been trapped in a snare in June that year. Its body was taken to a local vet, who photographed it, and it was then passed to a taxidermist. Unfortunately, it subsequently disappeared. Yet this story brought to light a further specimen, which had been shot the previous year close to the River Lossie near the village of Kellas in West Moray. Thomas Christie had seen cats of this type in the area before, and had decided to have this example stuffed and mounted in a ferocious pose after he had shot it. As a result, it was christened the Kellas cat.

A detailed examination of this specimen was carried out at the British Museum (Natural History) in London. Dr Daphne Hills concluded that in size it resembled a large wild cat, and while there was no previous record of a melanistic wild cat from Britain, they had been documented elsewhere within the species' range. Her conclusion was that, although it may have been a feral cat or a hybrid between a domestic cat and a wild cat, it seemed most likely that the Kellas cat was actually a melanistic wild cat. Other experts agreed, although a complete specimen had yet to be obtained at this stage. Certain bones, and the soft tissues, were not available in the case of the Kellas cat.

Then, during April 1985, another example was shot by a gamekeeper, about 16 km (10 miles) north of where the cat which triggered the interest had originally been obtained. This proved to be a young male, estimated to be about a year old. It was almost identical to the existing specimen, although it did have slight barring on the tail and the upper legs.

In this instance, more detailed study of the cranial structure was possible, and suggested that this individual had more features in common with a domestic cat. Even so, the museum experts concluded that the Avie cat, as it became known, was again more closely allied to the Scottish wild cat.

Chromosomal study was clearly vital if their precise relationships were to be resolved, but it would require a live specimen or one which had only recently died. It was hoped that another of these black cats, again shot close to Kellas, would provide the answer. Blood was taken by a veterinary surgeon soon after its death, but it proved to be contaminated and so was of no value.

The problem of identification became further complicated by a BBC television documentary, which initially appeared to provide the answer. A special trap had been used to capture what was originally believed to be a living specimen of the Kellas cat. A blood sample was then obtained, for chromosomal analysis at the University of Aberdeen. The result was clear-cut. This specimen was a hybrid between a wild cat and a domestic cat. Yet Edward Orbell, who has cared for this cat at the Highland Wildlife Park near Aviemore, is convinced that it is not a true representative of the Kellas cat. He had previously studied the first reported specimen which was the subject of the original newspaper article, and so was well placed to comment. Other scientists were equally unconvinced. This cat differed in its physical appearance, having a shorter, stouter body as well as significantly shorter teeth.

The situation became more confused with the capture in February 1988 of a cat which more closely resembled the accepted form of the Kellas cat. It was taken in a trap at Redcastle, in the north of Scotland. Further studies are still going on, using tissue samples taken from the preserved remains of some of the dead specimens. These may help to settle the debate about the status which should be accorded to these mysterious black cats.

As it appears at present, there could be four possibilities. First, the Kellas cat might prove to be an isolated population of feral cats. It is known that the black coloration can be linked genetically to an increase in size, which may explain why these cats are larger than feral cats elsewhere in the country. Yet there is further anatomical evidence, ranging from body shape to gut length, which suggests that these cats differ significantly from domestic cats, even when the latter have become feral. The wide distribution of Kellas cats also makes this explanation unlikely, especially when considered against feral cat populations in the Scottish Isles. If they were indeed feral, they would be likely to cover a wider area.

Although domestic cats have been widely introduced to islands around the world, and of necessity have an isolated distribution as a result, no similar change in their appearance corresponding to that of the Kellas cat has been noted. It seems even less likely that this would have occurred in Scotland, where domestic cats are prevalent and wild cats can also be found.

A more likely explanation is that the Kellas cat is the result of hybridization between wild and domestic or possibly even feral cats. Hybrids are well documented, with the number of feral cats in the region appearing to have peaked during the 1940s. Black coloration could subsequently have become quite widely dispersed in the population. However there is no consistency in the appearance of Kellas cats, either in their coloration or in their physical features.

Some, such as the one captured by the BBC, seem to be most closely related to

97

domestic cats, whereas others are of a distinctly different type. This situation could arise as the result of random pairings, following the initial matings, with some individuals diverging more closely towards one parent than the other over successive generations. Clearly, if matings with feral cats predominated, then the black individuals in that area would tend to resemble domestic rather than wild cats in appearance.

This variation tends to rule out the possibility that Kellas cats are simply a black variant of the wild cat, although there is some evidence which supports this theory. The small white throat patch has been recognized for over four hundred years as a distinctive feature of the wild cat. The absence of markings is also not particularly significant, because in other cats where a melanistic form is well recognized, as in the leopard for example, a few individuals lack the characteristic patterning associated with the species.

Harder to reconcile is the apparent divergence in physical features between wild cats and Kellas cats. While the limbs of the Kellas are longer, the tail has become shorter, for example. Even more significant, perhaps, are reported differences in the behaviour of these cats. Kellas cats have been seen in pairs, hunting during the day, which is a characteristic of domestic cats. Wild cats in contrast are generally solitary, preferring to hunt at first light and dusk, and may take larger prey. They are adept at climbing, which does not appear to be a feature of Kellas cat, and also lack their graceful running style, having a more compact gait. A particular oddity reported in the case of the Kellas cat is its apparent readiness to swim; it has even been seen catching fish in the River Lossie.

Dr Karl Shuker suggests that, bearing in mind its behavioural characteristics, the Kellas cat could represent the wild cat developing into a cursorial form, adept at running down prey in a similar fashion to the cheetah. Certainly, these cats possess a number of essential characteristics, which summarize the differences between them and the Scottish wild cat. A small head, with a thin body and relatively long legs, coupled with powerful hindquarters to provide thrust, are all features of the Kellas cat. All cursorial carnivores are defined on the basis of hind limb length relative to that of the vertebral column. The hind limbs need to be in excess of 80 per cent of the backbone length, and the measurements of the Kellas cat allow it to come into this category.

While investigating the mystery surrounding the Kellas cat, Dr Shuker uncovered an interesting earlier parallel. Black cats have been recorded in the region of Transcaucasia, in the former Soviet Union. They were first described by Professor Satunin in 1904, on the basis of three skulls and skins as well as two mounted specimens, and were accorded the scientific name of *Felis daemon*. Later, it was assumed that they were simply a feral form of the domestic cat.

There is, however, a marked similarity between these cats and the Kellas cat. Both have long white guard hairs scattered through their otherwise dark-coloured coat. Their head and body measurements are quite similar, although the tail lengths of these Transcaucasian black cats are longer than those of either the Kellas cat or Scottish wild cat. There have been no further reports of such cats from Transcaucasia in recent years, however, so no further research into their origins can be carried out. There is always the possibility that further specimens may be recorded in the future which could help to resolve the mystery.

African wild cat *Felis lybica*

DISTRIBUTION
The entire African continent and much of the Middle East, although absent from part of West Africa.

Although it has been suggested that the African wild cat should be regarded not as a separate species, but rather as a race of the European wild cat, this view is not universally accepted. There does appear to be a distinctive gap in the distribution of these cats, with the European form extending to the Caucasus, while its African counterpart does not occur further north than the Middle East in the western part of its range.

The African wild cat shows a variation in coloration through its range. Although in some instances stripes may be apparent they can be relatively inconspicuous, or might even be broken into spots, showing a patterning rather like that of a domestic spotted tabby.

The African wild cat is regarded as the ancestor of today's domestic cats. It displays a different temperament from the European form and is often found close to towns and other settlements, whereas the European wild cat avoids contact with people and is much more secretive by nature. Even the kittens of the European wild cat remain instinctively wild, whereas those of the African form can become quite tame, especially if they are hand-reared. In appearance, the African form is somewhat larger and stockier in build than its European counterpart.

African wild cats are found in a wide variety of habitats in both open and wooded country, and sometimes in mountainous regions. In some parts of their range, such as West Africa, different colour forms may be seen in the same area. Here, these cats may have steel-grey body coloration or a greyish tan, offset with reddish stripes. As a general rule, those living in arid areas have the lightest

Distribution of the
African wild cat
(*Felis lybica*).

99

coloured coats. The fur of these cats is also shorter than that of the European wild cat, presumably because of climatic differences. Their tails are longer, too, and taper along their length.

Their prey varies greatly according to the locality, but in general African wild cats feed predominantly on rodents; however they will also take insects, birds and other quarry. Breeding habits are similar to its European relative, with the gestation period lasting about sixty-five days. The kittens are mature at a year old.

Interestingly, the wild cats found on the Mediterranean islands are of African rather than European lineage. It seems likely that the Majorcan wild cat (*Felis lybica jordansi*) is already extinct, although a few unconfirmed sightings have been made in recent years. The problem of accurate identification is hampered because of the large population of feral cats on the island. The status of the wild cat population on Crete is almost equally in doubt because of hybridization. Other islands with wild cats include both Sardinia and Sicily, where the race *Felis lybica sarda* is very similar to the African mainland form.

The Corsican wild cat is perhaps the most mysterious of the cats from this region, because it is only documented from studies carried out in 1929. While L. Lavauden was investigating reports of a lynx on the island, a teacher brought him the skin and skull of a wild cat. It had been killed in the Forêt d'Aunes, south of Bastia.

The creature differed significantly from the Sicillian and Sardinian form: it had a much shorter tail and its coat was very dark, as could be expected from a forest-dwelling cat. It also lacked the russet tinge on the hair behind the ears. The distinctive feature of African wild cats, a black mark on the soles of the hind feet, continuing between the toes, was, however, apparent. This suggested to Lavauden that the cat was more closely related to the African than to the European races.

A further two skins were later obtained from the same source, but no further specimens have subsequently been reported. The skins themselves were passed to the Musée de Grenoble at Isère. The warden of the area, a Monsieur Rotges, confirmed that these cats were not apparently rare at that time. They could be seen not only in forested upland areas, but also in more open country. Since then, however, it appears likely that this race has become extinct.

In mainland Africa the African wild cat is declining in some areas, notably in the north, but it remains quite common further south. Populations in Central Asia are also reputedly good, because of the relative inaccessibility of the region. Their adaptability is partly a reflection of their diet. These cats have even been known to eat olives in times of drought.

African golden cat *Felis aurata*

DISTRIBUTION
Extends across Central Africa, from Senegal eastwards to the Mau forest of Kenya.

The coloration of these cats is highly variable, in spite of their name. Although it is normally a golden brown shade, individuals which have a greyish ground colour are not unknown; melanistic forms have also been documented. The

Distribution of the
African golden cat
(*Felis aurata*).

pattern of spotting may also differ markedly between individuals: some appear largely unspotted, while at the other extreme there can be dense spotting over the entire body, rather than just the legs and underparts. A dark central line running down the tail is characteristic. The African golden cat is about twice as large as a domestic cat.

When these cats were first described in 1827, it was believed that the colour forms were two different species: one was known as the golden cat, while the grey form was referred to as the silver cat. In fact, these colours can be seen throughout the range. More recent studies have shown that the coat patterns give a clearer insight into the origins of a particular specimen. Golden cats which are either heavily spotted, or have indistinct spots on their back and neck, occur only in West Africa; other forms are seen in the central and eastern parts of the species' range.

Considerable mythology surrounds these cats in certain areas of their range. In parts of Cameroon pygmy tribesmen value its tail as a talisman to protect them when they are hunting elephants. The skin is traditionally incorporated into tribal robes, and so highly valued locally that it is not usually traded.

Relatively little has been recorded about the habits of the African golden cat, although it appears to frequent high deciduous forest areas, and also the fringes of savannah in Guinea. It occurs at altitudes of up to 3600 m (12,000 ft) and is most active at dawn and dusk. African golden cats are sometimes known locally as the 'leopard's brother' since they inhabit similar country, and are reputed to be highly aggressive, at least when cornered. They are solitary by nature, and are capable of hunting both on the ground and in trees.

African golden cats are known to raid native villages on occasions, seizing poultry. They probably prey on other birds, tree hyraxes and assorted rodents. It is also likely that these cats sometimes take dinkers and other small antelopes.

Virtually nothing is known about their status. Recent studies, however, suggest that they may be relatively common in the Azagny and Tai National Parks in the Ivory Coast, and at some localities in Uganda.

The African golden cat (*Felis aurata*), like many cats, is solitary by nature. If often overlaps through its range with the leopard, but is much smaller in size.

The breeding habits of the African golden cat have not been documented from the wild, but this species has been bred successfully in captivity. The gestation period lasts about seventy-five days, after which just one or two kittens are born. Their development is relatively fast, with their eyes opening just a week after birth. At a fortnight old they are able to clamber around, and soon afterwards they have sufficient co-ordination to enable them to start jumping. Weaning begins when they are about six weeks old, and they start breeding about eighteen months later.

Asian golden cat *Felis temmincki*

DISTRIBUTION
Extends across South-east Asia, from Nepal and Tibet, eastwards via Assam, Burma, Thailand, Vietnam, Cambodia and Malaysia to southern China and Sumatra.

Sometimes described as Temminck's cat, this species shows certain similarities with the African golden cat, although their habitats are separated by a distance of some 7000 km (4300 miles). It is possible that their distribution may have been continuous in the past, before climatic changes intervened and led to arid conditions spreading through the Middle East.

During the Pleistocene epoch, some 2 million years ago, the weather in this part of the world was decidedly wetter than it is today, and tropical forests extended right across Africa to the Indian Ocean. Declining rainfall then resulted in eastern Africa becoming drier, and the forests were largely replaced by scrubland. This is likely to have resulted in the gradual separation of the African and Asian forms of the golden cat, and their evolution into distinct species.

The coloration of the Asian golden cat is as variable as that of its African counterpart. It can range from golden brown via golden red and dark brown to shades of grey, and is generally not heavily marked, although some individuals have a spotted belly. The distinctive subspecies sometimes called Fontainer's cat (*Felis temmincki tristis*), which occurs in the northern part of the range in areas of Burma and Tibet, is, however, heavily marked, with spots and sometimes stripes as well. It resembles the leopard cat (see p. 105), but is significantly larger. Melanistic individuals are not uncommon in this species, and have been kept in zoological collections. .

The Asian golden cat is slightly heavier than its African relative and occurs in similar habitat, preferring forested country. It frequents stretches of woodland broken with rocky outcrops, which has led to it becoming known as *shilului* – 'rock cat' – in China, and also *huang poo* or 'yellow leopard'.

Very little has been recorded about these cats in the wild, although they are known to prey on birds and, according to some reports, may climb trees. Other

Asian golden cat (*Felis temmincki*) – the coloration and patterning of these cats is variable through their range, and melanistic individuals are not uncommon. As with their African relative, their ground coloration is not necessarily golden.

Distribution of the Asian golden cat (*Felis temmincki*).

animals, for instance hares and small deer such as muntjac, are killed on the ground. Asian golden cats will also take domestic livestock, including goats and sheep, and occasionally young water buffalo calves. It is not clear whether the cat hunts during the day or at night.

Breeding, at least in some parts of its range, occurs early in the year and kittens can be born in February. These cats are reputed to use hollow trees as their dens, but may equally favour caves and other suitable retreats. Up to three kittens form a typical litter. Young Asian golden cats appear to tame quite readily when obtained at an early age, displaying considerable affection towards their owners. There is a record of one such individual which played with both domestic cats and dogs; it would go off hunting on its own, yet never failed to come back when it was called.

These cats have been hunted for their fur in some parts of their range, but now deforestation represents the greatest threat to their survival. Although there is no detailed knowledge about their numbers, they are thought to be endangered, at least in some areas.

Bay cat *Felis badia*

DISTRIBUTION
Confined to the island of Borneo, off the south-eastern coast of Asia.

This species resembles the Asian wild cat, although it is smaller. It occurs in two colour phases, one of which is bright reddish brown and has given rise to its alternative common name, the Bornean red cat. Spots may be present on the underparts, which are paler in colour, and on the limbs. There is also a greyer form which – like the brown variant – has pale white stripes extending on to the forehead and cheeks; the ears are covered with blackish brown hair. The tail is white on its lower surface, towards the tip, which is also white and has a black

Distribution of the bay cat (*Felis badia*).

spot. The bay cat has an unexplained anatomical peculiarity: its first upper pre-molar is smaller than normal, and only has one root. It has a short, rounded head.

One of the least known of all wild cats, this species is said to inhabit rocky limestone areas on forest borders, ranging up to an altitude of 900 m (3000 ft). Another report, however, suggests that the bay cat is an inhabitant of dense jungle.

It is reputed to feed on a variety of small mammals and birds, and will also eat carrion. The bay cat is said to be very fierce and can catch monkeys in the trees. Nothing else has been discovered to date about its lifestyle or indeed its numbers. But bearing in mind the widespread deforestation taking place in this part of the world there must be concern about the future of the species, especially in view of its very limited distribution.

Leopard cat *Felis bengalensis*

DISTRIBUTION
Occurs from India and Pakistan eastwards via the southern Himalayas and Bangladesh to Burma, Thailand, Vietnam, the Philippines, Malaysia south to Indonesia, and northwards as far as mainland China.

This attractively marked species is about the size of a domestic cat, but with slightly longer legs. It has a relatively small head and narrow muzzle. Again, the coloration of the coat varies through its range; the ground colour can be a pale yellow or tawny shade, reddish or grey. The black spots are generally numerous and may overlap, particularly on the flanks and at the back of the neck, to form discrete stripes. The underparts are white, and there are also white spots on the back of the ears, surrounded by darker areas of fur.

As would be expected, there is also considerable variation in leopard cats from differing parts of their range; the island races are among the most distinctive.

The Philippine race (*Felis bengalensis minutus*) is the smallest, while the largest forms are found on the mainland, along the northern edge of their distribution in Manchuria. These are also greyer, with thicker fur and less clearly defined spotted markings.

Bornean leopard cats (*Felis bengalensis borneoensis*) have a distinctly reddish hue to their fur, while those from Java (*Felis bengalensis javaensis*) are much duller in coloration. The Sumatran race (*Felis bengalensis sumatranus*) shows fewer markings than the mainland subspecies.

As might be expected, the leopard cat is an adaptable species. It is likely to be encountered in a wide variety of habitats, from taiga forest in the case of the Manchurian race (*Felis bengalensis manchurica*) to dense tropical forest and even agricultural land. Leopard cats do not stray far from water, however, and so are less likely to be encountered in very arid areas. They are also most common at low altitudes, and apparently do not range above 3000 m (10,000 ft).

These cats may use hollow trees or cavities under the roots for their den, as well as caves and other suitable retreats. They are essentially nocturnal, but may be seen on occasions during the day, especially away from human habitation. Their prey varies from rodents and other small mammals such as rabbits up to musk

The leopard cat (*Felis bengalensis*) is known to the Chinese as *chin-ch'ien mao*, which translates as money cat, because of the apparent similarity of its markings to Chinese coins.

Distribution of the leopard cat (*Felis bengalensis*).

deer and muntjac. They also eat birds, frequently stealing chickens if the opportunity presents itself. In parts of Siberia, leopard cats have been recorded eating both reptiles and fish. They are good swimmers, and adults also use water to conceal their faeces.

Leopard cats are solitary, except during the breeding period when a number of males may track a female. There seems to be no fixed mating period for these cats, especially in the southern part of their range. In Siberia, however, most kittens are born in the early summer – during late May the climate is most favourable to their survival.

Oestrus lasts between five and nine days, with gestation taking approximately nine to ten weeks. Two or three kittens form the usual litter, and they will remain within the relative safety of the den until they are about a month old.

Unfortunately in recent years, as greater protection has been given to the smaller New World cats, so the number of leopard cats being trapped for their skins has risen significantly. This was triggered in part by the removal in 1985 of the Chinese race, *Felis bengalensis bengalensis*, from CITES Appendix I, and its transfer to Appendix II, which allows regulated trade (see p. 13).

China has since become the major supplier of skins to the fashion market in Europe until imports were prohibited in 1987, and subsequently to Japan. A maximum export quota of 150,000 skins was set in 1989, when the total Chinese population of leopard cats was assessed at $1-1\frac{1}{2}$ million. Even so, there is real concern that trade may be more than the population can sustain, because in 1989 China had stockpiles of as many as 800,000 skins. It has been suggested that nearly 2 million of these cats were killed between 1985 and 1988, with the majority taken in Guizhou and Yunnan in the south-west of the country.

In other parts of their range leopard cats are protected, although they have become scarce in Pakistan, allegedly because of past over-exploitation for the skin trade. Their numbers may also have declined in India, where they are persecuted for killing poultry. Elsewhere, in the more southerly parts of their range especially, they are still regarded as quite numerous.

The range of this species has also recently been enlarged by the discovery of the Tshushima cat, named after the island where it was first found in 1988. With a total area of just 700 sq km (270 sq miles), this small island, lying between South Korea and Japan, is home to fewer than a hundred of these cats.

Professor Yuiti Ono, based at Kyushu University in Japan, describes this race of the leopard cat as relatively small, and dark in coloration. It is now considered to be the same form as the Manchurian race, *Felis bengalensis manchurica*. Males weigh around 4 kg (10 lb), while females are about 1 kg (2.2 lb) lighter on average.

The occurrence of the Tshushima cat suggests that its ancestors originated from mainland Asia, but that it has since become isolated. The leopard cat only extends into North Korea, being absent further south, nor does it occur in Japan. Professor Ono believes that the pine forests growing in limestone areas offer little prey for these cats, which is why leopard cats no longer occur throughout Korea.

Tshushima Island is mountainous, with deep ravines, and seems ideal habitat for the cats. They are not harassed by the local people, who tend to be either fishermen or mushroom farmers. Although there are feral cats on the island, they do not seem to be breeding with the Tshushima cat itself. It may be seen quite close to villages, though, as well as in the vicinity of paddy fields and around the edge of forests.

The diet and habits of the Tshushima cat are still unknown, but probably do not differ significantly from those of other leopard cats. Its future may be relatively secure, in spite of its low numbers, because it is not suffering persecution, and the topography of the island means that widespread development is unlikely to take place here.

Iriomote cat *Felis iriomotensis*

DISTRIBUTION
Confined to the island of Iriomote, Japan.

First described in 1967 by Dr Imaizumi of the National Science Museum in Tokyo, the Iriomote cat has been the subject of taxonomic dispute ever since. He considered it to be a representative of a feline lineage which was thought to have become extinct, and ascribed it to a new genus, *Mayailurus*. More recently, it has been suggested that this cat should be grouped as a subspecies of the leopard cat, especially following the discovery of the Tshushima cat in the same part of the world.

A palaeontologist called Dr Haseqawa has uncovered fossil remains on the nearby island of Miyakojima, which suggest that the Iriomote cat has existed as a separate form for approximately 2 million years. Further support for the view that the Iriomote cat is a distinct species comes from investigations into its anatomy by Professor Paul Leyhausen. He points out that, although its skull structure does have a number of affinities with the leopard cat, it also possesses characteristics found in other species, including the marbled cat and both African and Asian golden cats.

In addition, there is a distinctive difference in the structure of its claws compared with those of the leopard cat. These are not entirely sheathed, while the toes themselves show partial webbing, which is a feature associated with the

Distribution of the iriomote cat (*Felis iriomotensis*).

fishing cat (see p. 111). The claws of the Iriomote cat also do not retract fully, as they do in the leopard cat. Another anatomical difference is that the bullae of its ears are small, which suggests that sight may be more significant than hearing when capturing prey.

The Iriomote cat is similar in size to the domestic cat, but tends to have shorter legs and tail. It is dark brown, with rows of darker spots running along the body. Between five and seven lines extend from the back of the neck to the shoulders. The ears are rounded, with dark fur on their backs, and a white spot in the centre. The tail is thick and bushy, with dark rings encircling it, and dark spots on the upper surface close to the base.

Iriomote island lies east of Taiwan and has a total area of just 292 sq km (113 sq miles). The cats inhabit both the mountainous areas, which are well wooded, and more open cultivated areas, as well as roaming along the beaches on occasion.

Although solitary by nature, these cats appear to establish individual territories, which can extend over an area of 2–3 sq km (0.8–1.2 sq miles) and these may be shared in part with other individuals; the boundaries are marked with urine. The low build of these cats enables them to move through quite dense undergrowth, especially if paths have previously been made by the wild boar which live here.

During the winter months, the cats appear to move down from the more remote mountainous regions to lower ground. They feed on a wide variety of prey including birds, rodents, fruit bats, reptiles, amphibians and crabs. The Iriomote cat is also able to swim well and catches fish, including mud skippers on the shore. It can climb well if needed, and may hunt off the ground quite regularly, especially at night.

The current population is estimated to be about a hundred at most, and although Iriomote cats are officially protected, native villagers sometimes hunt and eat them. They can also fall victim to traps left for other animals, particularly Ryukyu wild boar. Poisonous snakes may also represent a danger. Part of their habitat has, however, now been declared a National Park and wildlife protection area. Japan's Environment Agency has set up a feeding and monitoring programme for these cats on Iriomote, with a view to increasing their numbers.

Not much is known about the reproductive habits of this species, but it is thought that females usually give birth to between one and four kittens. Mating has been recorded in February and March, and again during September and October, so it is possible that two litters could be produced in a year. Fighting between males, prior to mating, has been documented. Pregnancy lasts about eight weeks and the female gives birth in a den which may be a hollow tree or under rocks. A partial albino form has been recorded, but this is the only known colour variant.

Fishing cat *Felis viverrina*

DISTRIBUTION
Occurs in isolated pockets of suitable habitat across Asia, from south-western India and Sri Lanka via the southern Himalayas, Bangladesh, Burma, Thailand and Vietnam into China and south to the islands of Sumatra and Java.

Its resemblance to a civet is what led to the fishing cat being christened *Felis viverrina*. It differs in some respects from other cats, being powerfully built but with a surprisingly short tail, which is less than a third of the combined head and body length. The tail is also particularly thick near its base, for reasons which are unclear. In overall size the fishing cat is larger than the leopard cat and duller in coloration, being greyish with dark brown spots running down its sides in rows. White spots are again apparent in the centre of the ears, with between six to eight dark lines extending from the forehead over the crown of the head and down the neck.

Distribution of the fishing cat (*Felis viverrina*).

While entering water regularly, and swimming well, the heavily-built fishing cat (*Felis viverrina*) will take a variety of other prey besides fish.

Webbing is apparent between the toes of the front feet, while the sheaths here are not large enough to accommodate the claws fully, so that they project even when the cat is walking. The extent of this webbing has recently been the subject of some debate; it has been suggested that it is no more extensive than in other species such as the bobcat, and so is not related to the aquatic habitat where these cats are found.

Fishing cats do not stray far from streams and rivers, preferring areas with good cover such as reed beds, mangrove swamps and marsh areas. They may range up to an altitude of 1500 m (5000 ft) in the Himalayas.

The English name for these cats is a literal translation of the Bengali *machbagral*, although for a period there was some doubt as to the significance of fish in their diet. It is now clear, however, that fish forms a major part of their food intake. A fishing cat will sit on a sandbank or rock, watching intently for passing fish which it will then scoop out of the water with one of its front paws. It will also wade into shallow water and may even dive in pursuit of a fish, grabbing it directly in its mouth.

Other prey, such as *Ampullaria* snails and crustaceans of various types, may be easier to gather in the shallows. Frogs and snakes are also eaten by fishing cats. On land, they will take birds and small mammals, and have been recorded as scavenging on the carcass of a dead cow.

These cats, which can weigh up to 12 kg (26½ lb), have a reputation for ferocity, and are said to be capable of driving off a pack of dogs when cornered. There is also a remarkable tale of a fishing cat which carried off a four-month-old baby at Jeypore. The cat was killed, and the infant returned safely to its mother. Similar stories from the western coastal area of India have been reported, so this may well not have been an isolated incident, although there is no report of any attacks on adults.

A further example of the strength of these cats followed the capture of a male, which was housed in an enclosure adjoining that of a female leopard. It broke through and killed the leopard, which was twice its size. Young fishing cat kittens prove quite tractable, however, and are usually friendly towards people whom they know well.

It is thought that fishing cats may breed throughout the year, at least in those parts of their range where conditions are favourable. At this stage the characteristic chirping calls uttered by both sexes may be heard, with mating most likely in February and August. The gestation period lasts for just over two months, after which two or three kittens are born in a den which may be concealed in reed beds.

While male fishing cats, distinguishable by their larger size, will assist in the rearing of kittens born in captivity, it is not clear whether they participate in this way in the wild. Kittens are born blind, and their eyes open when they are just over two weeks old. They leave the den for the first time when they are about one month old, and are starting to eat solid food approximately a month later. The young cats are fully grown by nine months old.

The wide distribution of the fishing cat is deceptive when it comes to assessing their numbers, simply because of their specialist requirements in terms of habitat. Overall they are thought to be endangered and so feature on CITES Appendix I (see p. 13). In India the species is still widely distributed, however, and present in a number of reserves. But hunting for its coat is a problem in various countries, including India, and this persecution has brought it to the verge of extinction in Pakistan. Poisoning and habitat destruction are also threats in Bangladesh and elsewhere.

Flat-headed cat *Felis planiceps*

DISTRIBUTION
Thailand, Malaysian peninsula, Indonesia, Sumatra and Borneo.

This, the most distinctive of all the smaller cats, is similar in size to a domestic cat. Its head is broad and flat, with small ears set well down on the sides of the elongated skull. The eyes are large, while the legs are relatively short, as is the tail. Its fur is thick, soft and reddish brown, usually with a silvery tinge. The underparts in contrast are white with brown spots, and two clearly defined white stripes run from the sides of the nose up to the forehead.

The claws of the flat-headed cat are not entirely retractable, with the result that their tips remain visible even when the claws are retracted. Their pattern of dentition is unique in that all their teeth are pointed; the upper pre-molar is particularly strong, being anchored into the jaw by two roots.

Distribution of the flat-headed cat (*Felis planiceps*).

Very little is known about the flat-headed cat. It appears to be largely nocturnal and has been observed at altitudes up to 700 m (2300 ft). Fish, frogs and other aquatic creatures figure prominently in its diet, and these cats occasionally get caught in fish traps. They have also been known to pursue chickens, and supposedly, according to a nineteenth-century report, are very destructive in gardens: they were reputed to dig up sweet potatoes and plunder fruit.

The rather unusual shape of their heads may make it easier for them to catch fish, as do the sharp teeth in their jaws. Many zoologists feel that this species is actually better equipped than the fishing cat for aquatic hunting, and it invariably occurs close to water.

A young flat-headed kitten was found in January, but nothing is known about their courtship or mating behaviour. Another kitten, reared on a diet of eggs, milk and prawns, became very tame. Its coat coloration changed from grey to light brown as it matured. While it later ate fish avidly, it ignored rice. Litter size in the flat-headed cat may be slightly larger than in similar species, however, since the female has two pairs of nipples rather than one, which is more common in the smaller felids.

The status of this cat is also essentially a matter for speculation. It does not appear to be common, and in both Indonesia and Thailand this species could well be endangered. It is afforded protection from international trade by being listed on CITES Appendix I (see p. 13), but it does not appear to have been seriously persecuted at any stage for its fur.

Its secretive lifestyle means that much still remains to be learnt about the flat-headed cat's habits, as well as its status. It could be that the flat-headed cat is more common than previously believed, although it would also seem fairly certain that its distribution is closely linked to the availability of suitable stretches of water.

Jungle cat *Felis chaus*

DISTRIBUTION

Extends from Egypt north-eastwards through Jordan and the Middle East to the borders of the Caspian Sea and Afghanistan, ranging further east via India, Nepal, Sri Lanka, Burma and Thailand to south-western China.

Since the jungle cat occurs across such a wide area there are noticeable differences in the appearance of these cats, which to some extent reflects their varied habitat. They are found in areas of jungle, as their name implies; but in Egypt, for example, they also often inhabit reed beds. The subspecies occurring here is known as the reed cat (*Felis chaus nilotica*) or swamp cat. There are also distinct variations in weight: jungle cats originating in Central Asia tend to be much heavier than individuals from Thailand or neighbouring areas, and weigh up to 16 kg (36 lb). Where their distributions overlap, jungle cats can be easily separated from the African wild cat on the basis of size: the former are noticeably larger and have longer legs.

The jungle cat's ground coloration can vary from sandy yellow through red to shades of grey. In general terms, jungle cats from the north of their range have a greyer coat than those occurring in more southerly and eastern parts. There are no markings on the body, apart from brown stripes on the legs and similar rings around the tail, which has a dark tip. A number of melanistic individuals have been reported, notably from India and Pakistan, dating back to 1912.

Distribution of the jungle cat (*Felis chaus*).

The jungle cat's essentially unmarked coat is a feature of this group of cats, although their coloration can vary from reddish through to grey.

The ears of the jungle cat are tipped with tufts of black hair, and are relatively tall and rounded. Keen hearing helps them to locate prey in dense areas of vegetation. These cats may be seen in a wide variety of habitats, including open grassland and agricultural areas, although they avoid desert and rainforest. They have been observed at altitudes of 2400 m (8000 ft) in the Himalayas, and are not especially shy of people. In Kashmir they have even been recorded sleeping in buildings, and may often enter villages without being detected.

Jungle cats are frequently active during the daytime, and will take over a den excavated and abandoned by another animal, such as a fox, retreating here either to rest or if danger threatens. They may use several in their territory. Their hunting technique varies according to the area concerned, with the cat using available cover to creep up on unsuspecting prey. They move quietly at a slow trot, before bounding forward at considerable pace when necessary, reaching a speed equivalent to 23 kph (14 mph). Rats, mice, hares and other small mammals are favoured prey, while the ability of these cats to jump vertically into the air helps them to catch game birds such as pheasants and francolins, possibly seizing them in the air as they try to fly off.

Jungle cats are very catholic in their feeding preferences. They will kill porcupines, and may then take over their burrows as well. They are also powerful enough to prey on the fawns of axis deer, and will eat snakes and frogs. In Tadzhikistan, jungle cats have even been known to consume olives, but in spite of the fact that they are capable of climbing they prefer to remain on the ground. These cats can also swim well if necessary.

The breeding period is variable, and influenced by the locality. In northern parts of their range jungle cats mate in February and March, with males calling loudly at this stage. Further south, in India for example, they appear able to breed throughout the year.

The oestrus period lasts about five days, with one or more males stalking a potential mate from a distance until she is ready to accept their attentions. Three or four kittens are born about eight weeks later, sometimes in a snug nest hidden in reed beds and lined with fur, rather than in an underground burrow. It is believed that, at least in some parts of their range, females may produce two litters of kittens during the year. Their litter size is also quite variable, and can comprise as many as seven.

Kittens differ significantly in appearance from adults, becuase they have very distinctive black tabby markings on their coats and are also greyer overall. These stripes may initially offer camouflage, and gradually disappear as they grow older. The kittens will start to be weaned around eight weeks old, and then separate from their mother about three months later, by which time their coloration largely resembles that of the adult jungle cat. They are likely to be mature by the age of eighteen months.

There has long been speculation as to whether the jungle cat played a part in the development of the domestic cat. Certainly, these cats were tamed and trained by the ancient Egyptians to hunt wildfowl. They also featured in the art of the period, and their mummified remains have been discovered in tombs from this era which show that they occupied a place in the Egyptians' affections.

Even so, it is generally accepted that this larger species did not play a part, yet its coloration is not unlike that of the contemporary Abyssinian breed, being what is described by cat fanciers as a ticked tabby. Another characteristic feature of the Abyssinian cat, particularly favoured in show circles, is the presence of lynx-like ear tufts. These are clearly evident in the jungle cat, but not in the African wild cat. This possibility cannot therefore be dismissed entirely.

Pallas's cat *Felis manul*

DISTRIBUTION

Ranges eastwards from the borders of the Caspian Sea and Iran to western China, central Kazakhstan, the Altai Mountains and Inner Mongolia, reaching Tibet and Ladakh.

Although apparently present over a broad area, these cats are actually scarce or absent in many parts of their range. Named after the German naturalist Peter Pallas, who discovered it in the vicinity of the Caspian Sea in the eighteenth century, this species is also known as the manul.

Its appearance is quite distinctive. These cats resemble the domestic cat in size, but have a shorter and much broader head, with very small ears set low down on the sides of the head. Their eyes are large and owl-like, while the heavy body is supported on short, stocky legs.

Their coat is longer than that of any other species of cat, and may vary in colour from light grey to yellowish brown and russet. The frosted appearance of

Distribution of the Pallas's cat (*Felis manul*).

the coat is caused by the white tips to the hairs. It is the fur on the underparts which is longest – about double the length of that on the rest of the body. There are also two dark stripes extending across the cheeks, while stripes may also be evident on the limbs and hindquarters. Dark rings encircle the tail. The chin, as well as the lips and the throat area, are white.

Pallas's cat inhabits arid and inhospitable part of the world, and its long, dense fur provides insulation against the freezing winter temperatures. It can be found in both steppe and desert, and has been observed on rocky plateaux up to an altitude of 4000 m (13,000 ft). These cats are secretive and solitary by nature, which makes it difficult to study their habits. In the southern area of the Altai, Pallas's cat may be found close to the rocky streams known as *kurumiks*. It hides away for much of the day in caves or hollows under stones, or may adopt the burrows of other creatures such as marmots.

The distinctive appearance of Pallas's cat helps it to merge into the background in its habitat of relatively open country. The low-set ears are not very conspicuous, while the forward-pointing eyes, set quite high in the skull, give good vision even when the head itself is kept low. Cats have what is known as a nictitating membrane in the corner of each eye nearest to the nose. In Pallas's cat this 'third' eyelid is well developed and may afford protection against the dust storms which arise in parts of their range, while their short limbs enable them to climb very effectively.

These cats emerge from their hiding places at dusk and prefer to hunt at night, although they may occasionally be seen during the daytime as well. They appear to rely heavily on their sense of sight to locate prey, which often consists of pikas, marmots and other small mammals. Mice are relatively insignificant in their diet, particularly in some areas.

Their mating calls have variously been described as resembling either a small dog barking, or the screech of an owl. At close quarters they may utter a shrill call when under threat, keeping their lips almost completely closed.

In some parts of the species' range breeding occurs early in the year, and kittens are born in April and May. In captivity litters may comprise up to six kittens, which each weigh between 70 and 100 g (2.5–3.5 oz) at birth, after a gestation period of about nine weeks. The kittens have a thick, woolly coat and lack the white tips to the hairs which create the frosted appearance seen in adults.

These cats are said to remain intractable, but certainly there are reliable accounts of them becoming quite tame. One kept by a Colonel E. Ward, obtained from Ladakh, was friendly towards him but reserved with strangers. Pallas himself recorded that they would hybridize with domestic cats, and suggested that these cats may have been involved in the original development of long-haired breeds, which began in the vicinity of the Caspian Sea, possibly in Turkey

Although this view is not given any credence by zoologists today, there are no records of trial pairings being made in the two hundred years since Pallas put forward his theory. It is hard to gain a reliable insight into the numbers of Pallas's cats through their wide range. In some areas, notably northern India and parts of the former USSR, they are believed to have declined; but elsewhere, in China and Mongolia, the species is thought to be quite numerous. The fur of Pallas's cat is sometimes sold in China, but it is supposedly protected because it kills rodents.

Chinese desert cat *Felis bieti*

DISTRIBUTION
From south-western China, it extends from the eastern Tibetan plateau via central Sichuan northwards to Gansu in inner Mongolia.

In spite of its name this cat does not inhabit an area of desert, but is found in steppeland and mountainous areas where cover is available in the form of shrubs or sparse forests. Again about the size of a domestic cat, it is predominantly yellowish grey but darker on its back. Brownish fur may sometimes be apparent on the cheeks, flanks and haunches. The pads are well protected, with long hair between the toes, but this is not as profuse as in the sand cat. There are also short tufts of hair, approximately 2 cm (0.8 in) long, on the ears. The tail is ringed with three or four prominent black bands, and has a black tip.

This species was first known from a skin obtained in a Chinese fur market in 1899. Its entirely fortuitous discovery was made when Prince Henry d'Orleans, who was leading a scientific expedition to the region, was prohibited by the authorities from entering the sacred Tibetan city of Lhasa. He then had to travel east, in the direction of Sichuan, where a member of his party found two furs on sale which could not be identified. These remained the sole source of knowledge about the existence of these cats, until a skull was acquired in 1925. Subsequently very little has been documented about these cats, although it is known that they may range up to an altitude of at least 3000 m (10,000 ft). A dog is reported to have been attacked and bitten by one of these cats, after chasing it.

Nothing is known about the habits of the Chinese desert cat at present, nor is its status clear. It is not protected in China, however, and is hunted for its fur. The presence of ear tufts, and the relatively large auditory vesicles in the skull, suggest that these cats rely heavily on their hearing for hunting purposes, although their prey is unknown. Presumably they eat bamboo rats and other rodents and birds found in this part of the world.

Distribution of the Chinese desert cat (*Felis bieti*).

Some zoologists have proposed that these cats are actually closely related to the wild cat. Further study may reveal that their status as a separate species is not actually justified, and that they should in fact be classified as an eastern race of the wild cat species.

Sand cat *Felis margarita*

DISTRIBUTION
Discontinuous, with five separate populations occurring in the Sahara area, from Algeria to Arabia, and south to Niger, as well as in Russian Turkestan and Pakistan.

Sometimes known as the sand dune cat, members of this species are relatively small, with short legs. The face is broad, with large, well-spaced ears set low on the head; the whiskers are particularly prominent. Their fur is soft and dense, ranging from sandy to light grey in ground coloration; it is typically darker across the back and whitish on the muzzle and chest. There is a characteristic reddish streak running across the cheeks from the corner of each eye. The ears themselves have a covering of tawny fur on their rear, and black tips. Black markings are also apparent elsewhere on the body; they are prominent on the limbs, with rings also encircling the tail which has a black tip.

The sand cat, as its name suggests, inhabits very arid areas, especially where there are sand dunes; it may also be seen in rocky terrain. The soles of the feet are well protected with dense mats of fur, measuring about 2 cm (0.8 in) long, which extend from between the toes and cover the pads. These protect the cat when it is walking on scorching desert sand. This thick padding of fur on the feet also enables it to walk effectively on loose, shifting sand without sinking into the ground. These cats use their powerful, short legs to dig burrows, where they can retreat when the sun is at its hottest during the day.

They prefer to hunt at night, becoming active at dusk. Sand cats have particularly acute hearing, and yet the low positioning of the ears on the head enables

Distribution of
the sand cat
(*Felis margarita*).

them to remain relatively inconspicuous in a region where little natural cover is available. Desert rodents such as jerboas form the bulk of their diet, but they may also catch lizards, hares, birds and invertebrates, notably locusts. The availability of metabolic water, derived from their food, and a very efficient urinary system means that these cats are apparently able to survive for long periods without drinking.

The sounds made by these cats are said to resemble those of domestic cats, although males make a loud barking call during the mating period. In some parts of their range kittens are born in April, but in captivity sand cats may breed throughout the year. Litters can comprise as many as eight kittens, although four appears to be the average. Their growth rate is staggering. Weighing about 39 g (1.4 oz) at birth, the young sand cats then gain approximately 12 g (0.4 oz) every day over the course of the next three weeks. They remain in the burrow at first, with their eyes opening when they are about two weeks old. At about five weeks the young kittens emerge from the burrow and start to display digging behaviour. These cats are essentially terrestrial by nature, and rarely climb. They will stay together as a group until they are at least four months old. The markings in young desert cats are more pronounced than in adults, and they will also still be slightly smaller when they separate.

All desert cats are vulnerable to venomous snakes, which may be tempted to investigate their burrows. If caught out in the open during the day, they may be seized by large birds of prey. Wolves can also pose a threat to them in some areas.

Sand cats appear to wander quite widely, which can make an accurate assessment of their numbers difficult. Even so, it appears that they are generally scarce, with the species considered endangered in Pakistan.

Black-footed cat *Felis nigripes*

DISTRIBUTION
Occurs in southern Africa, being widely distributed in Botswana, and in Namibia extending as far west as Quickborn near Okahandja. It is present in Cape Province, reaching Beaufort in the south, and has been observed eastwards in Orange Free State and Transvaal as well as Zimbabwe.

The name of these cats originates from the distinctive black markings on their pads. They are the smallest of all wild cats, and females may weight just 1.5 kg (3.25 lb). Their fur is yellowish brown, varying somewhat in shade between individuals, and marked with prominent black or brownish spots which extend in rows across the shoulders where they merge to form stripes. Prominent black barring is also evident on the legs, and the short tail too is ringed with these darker markings as well as having a black tip. The black-footed cats in Botswana are both darker in overall coloration and larger than those from elsewhere, and so have been recognized as a distinctive subspecies (*Felis nigripes thomasi*).

Black-footed cats inhabit dry, open country, and often take over the burrows of spring hares or use termite nests for their dens, which has led to them being known locally as anthill tigers. They also eat invertebrates quite regularly, as well as consuming grass.

Distribution of the
black-footed cat
(*Felis nigripes*).

Black-footed cats have acquired a reputation for ferocity: local folklore tells of their attacks on sheep by fastening on to the neck and piercing the jugular vein. This of course is a rather uncharacteristic method for cats to adopt and gains no further credence from tales told by Masarwa bushmen that these cats kill giraffes in a similar fashion!

Their most likely prey is ground squirrels, birds and even reptiles. Although these cats are said to be usually nocturnal, they may be observed during the day – certainly in the Kruger National Park. This behaviour may be linked to the level of persecution which they face, however – experience with other species has shown that they become bolder in national parks where they are free from hunting pressures.

There is also dispute as to whether black-footed cats are social, but it seems most likely that they are solitary. From observations of captive specimens it appears that males have larger territories than females, which are marked by urine spraying.

Births are most common during November and December, with the gestation period lasting approximately nine weeks. The oestrus phase is thought to be very short, lasting perhaps a single day with the female being receptive for between five and ten hours only. A male must therefore be in the immediate vicinity if successful mating is to take place, which gives some support to the view that these cats are not entirely anti-social. Contact is made easier by the loud mewing calls of this species, which are audible over some considerable distance.

The female will give birth typically to two kittens in an underground burrow. She may move them as they grow older, concealing them under bushes perhaps while she is hunting. They are all very much at risk from predators because of their small size.

The kittens are born with pink rather than black feet, with this characteristic coloration only becoming apparent when they are about six weeks old. They develop quite rapidly, and their eyes open by the time they are eight days old.

The black-footed cat (*Felis nigripes*) is the smallest of the African wild cats and occurs in arid areas of the continent.

Young black-footed cats may be able to walk at just two weeks of age, and a week later are likely to be venturing forth from the nest on their own.

They are running well by six weeks old, but tend to remain close to the mother. If danger threatens, they will scatter and freeze wherever they are, rather than attempting to stay alongside their den. Their mother then utters a quiet, low call and signals by raising and lowering her ears that it is safe for them to return to her.

Purring is a particular feature of the black-footed cat, and the young are able to purr from birth. They typically appear darker than adults, because at this early stage their markings predominate in the coat. The weaning process begins when they are about five weeks old, and kittens can be catching prey themselves within a further week.

Interestingly, although the initial development of black-footed cats is precocious when compared with domestic cats, their age of maturity is subsequently much delayed. It appears that they are unlikely to breed much before they are twenty-one months old. Studies suggest that these small cats are relatively numerous through their range, however, and even common in some areas. In captivity they have hybridized with domestic cats, and are recorded to have bred with a local subspecies of the African wild cat in southern Africa.

Rusty-spotted cat *Felis rubiginosa*

DISTRIBUTION

Found in Sri Lanka and southern India, but also recorded from Jammu and Gujarat in the north of India. Its principal centre of distribution on the mainland is in western India.

The name of this cat conveys a good impression of its appearance. It is predominantly greyish brown with a reddish suffusion to the fur, while the underparts are noticeably paler. Elongated rusty-brown spots are superimposed on this ground coloration, arranged in lines along the sides and the back, with blotches on the belly. Dark stripes extend up over the forehead, bordered by two prominent white bands which run adjacent to the eyes. There may also be some spots on the tail, and the soles of the feet are black. Two subspecies are recognized, with the race present on Sri Lanka, *Felis rubiginosa phillipsi*, having a more reddish tone. The rusty-spotted cat is similar in size to the black-footed cat.

   The discontinuous distribution of this species is rather mysterious, and a recent view is that these cats occur over a wider area of India than was previously

The rusty-spotted cat (*Felis rubignosa*) is the smallest of all felids, being only approximately half the size of the domestic cat. It appears to be largely arboreal. Youngsters are less distinctly marked than adults.

Distribution of the rusty-spotted cat (*Felis rubiginosa*).

thought. They were first photographed in the Gir Lion Sanctuary in western India in 1989. At present, its most northerly record comes from close to Udhampur in Jammu and Kashmir state. There have also been recent sightings from the Dangs forest in southern Gujarat.

The two races tend to occupy very different areas. The population on Sri Lanka inhabits forested areas and is restricted largely to the south of the island, in the humid, mountainous jungles. Rusty-spotted cats are not found in the drier, more open regions in the north. Conversely, in India they tend to be encountered in scrub and grassland rather than dense jungles, although they have been observed in some forested areas.

The reason for this division is unclear, but there is no doubting the opportunistic nature of the rusty-spotted cat. In a further extension to their range, a population has been discovered living in abandoned houses in southern India. This is a densely populated area, well away from the type of terrain where they are usually found, but the exact location is not being revealed in order to protect their presence. The houses have wooden ceilings and rafters beneath a tiled roof, while cultivated plants such as banana and mango trees grow in the vicinity. It is thought that the cats are catching rodents around the dwellings, and may also be taking nearby chickens as food.

Rusty-spotted cats are largely nocturnal, and relatively little is known about their behaviour. Tame individuals prove to be agile climbers, and they may steal nestlings or catch older birds in trees. They also appear to be quite territorial, spraying regularly at certain localities.

The breeding habits of this species are largely undocumented, but kittens are born in April. They are duller in coloration than adults, with less distinctive rusty spotting on the coat. Snakes may pose a threat to these small cats. If kittens are obtained at an early age, they will apparently develop into delightful pets and resemble domestic cats in their antics, proving just as affectionate towards people.

Serval *Felis serval*

DISTRIBUTION
Occurs in Algeria and Morocco, and south of the Sahara including Ethiopia, but not at the southern tip of the African continent.

Although the serval is found over a wide area of Africa, its range has contracted during recent times. Only a small population occurs in the northern region, it having disappeared from the vicinity of the Atlas Mountains at least twenty years ago. The subspecies which is found in North Africa, called *Felis serval constantina*, is considered endangered.

The physical appearance of these cats is very distinctive. They are tall, measuring 60 cm (24 in) at the shoulder, and have a relatively small head topped with a very large pair of ears. The tail in contrast is quite short, extending only to the level of the hocks.

The ground colour is yellowish buff over the the body, with whitish underparts. The coat has black markings which can vary greatly in size. They typically merge to form stripes covering the neck and extend down the sides of the chest, but there is considerable variation in appearance depending on the origins of the individual cat. Servals originating from grassland and relatively open country have larger spots than those occurring in forested areas. In the former, the spots typically merge along the back. They continue down the tail, becoming rings along its length, and the tip is invariably black. As in a number of other species, the backs of the ears are covered with black fur while the centres are white. Occasional melanistic servals are known, especially from East Africa in the vicinity of Kilimanjaro, Mount Kenya and elsewhere. Such cats are most likely to be encountered on the borders of rainforest and in highland areas.

It has long been assumed that servals were mainly nocturnal, but this has recently been disproved by a detailed four-year study carried out in the Ngorongoro Crater region of Tanzania. The servals here are crepuscular, preferring to hunt in the early morning or at dusk. They tend to rest mainly during the middle of the day, and for a shorter period at night. Dr Aadfe Geertsema's study

Distribution of
the serval
(*Felis serval*).

Servals (*Felis serval*) are often active during the day. These cats rely heavily on their sense of hearing when hunting, particularly when they are seeking small rodents in dense vegetation.

also revealed that female servals were more active than their male counterparts, particularly when they had kittens. These cats may also rest more during the dry season.

The serval hunts predominantly by relying on its sense of hearing to locate prey – it has very acute parabolic ears, which trap sound waves most effectively. Servals have a very distinctive hunting style as well, first listening intently to a rustle in the grass and locating its source with considerable precision. Then, judging the moment carefully, the cat will pounce on its prey. The impact may kill the unfortunate animal outright, or stun it, in which case the cat is likely to dispatch it with a neck bite.

Small rodents form the bulk of the diet, but these cats will also take birds as large as guinea fowl, plucking them before eating them. Young antelopes may fall victim to servals, as may lizards. Servals have been known to dig mole rats out from underground tunnels, having heard their movements beneath the soil.

The population of servals in the Ngorongoro Crater made nearly ten kills in each daylight period, achieving a kill rate of five animals or birds in a distance of 2 km (1.2 miles). This was marginally more profitable than hunting at night, where just six kills were typically made in the equivalent period, yet their strike rate was higher after dark, with just over half of their attempts being successful. These servals frequently fed on frogs as well as rodents. They also ate grass regularly, but rarely scavenged.

All servals in the study group were observed to use their urine for scent-marking, with the adult male spraying most often through the territory. Encounters with other servals invariably triggered renewed scent-marking, which was then more frequent for a period. The size of a serval's territory varies according to the availability of prey – males have a larger home range than females, which may be about 11.6 sq km (4.5 sq miles). Immature servals appear to be driven from one area to the next, and presumably they settle when they can find a territory of their own.

These cats have no fixed breeding period in the year, but oestrus is short, lasting just a day in most cases. Mating tends to peak during the spring, however, and this is the only time that these cats come together. Two or three kittens are likely to be born between ten and eleven weeks later. The den may be simply a hole under rocks, or even a secure area of dense scrub; sometimes the female will take over the abandoned burrow of another creature such as a porcupine. By eleven days old the kittens will have doubled their birth weight and are likely to be nearly weaned by the age of five months. They gain their permanent canine teeth in a further month, and separate to establish their own territory when they are around a year old.

Servals face few enemies in the wild, but are persecuted by people and some-times hunted with dogs. They can run fast over short distances, however, and bound into trees for security – they are capable of jumping nearly 3 m (10 ft) straight off the ground. This may be sufficiently off-putting for leopards, which also hunt them. Native people kill servals for food, and use their skins in tradi-tional fur cloaks called *karrosses*.

These are not particularly aggressive cats, and the accounts of those who have kept them indicate that they settle well into a domestic lifestyle. They purr like domestic cats and also communicate by means of high-pitched calls, which are presumably audible to other servals some distance away.

SMALL CATS OF THE NEW WORLD

Jaguarundi *Felis yagouaroundi*

DISTRIBUTION
Extends from southern Texas and Arizona in the USA southwards as far as Peru and north-west Argentina, east of the Andes. It also occurs in Paraguay and Brazil.

This is one of the least characteristic of all cats, resembling a cross between an otter and a weasel; indeed, its name in German translates as the 'weasel cat'. Its head is small and flattened, with broad, short and rounded ears. The body is long and slender and carried on short legs, while the tail is also relatively elongated, being up to 51 cm (20 in) in length.

The colour of its coat is very variable, but quite uniform in individuals. It can range from shades of grey, appearing almost melanistic in some cases, through chocolate and foxy red to deep chestnut. When these cats were first discovered, this marked difference in coloration led taxonomists to classify them as two distinct species. The grey form was recognized as the jaguarundi, with the reddish variant being called the eyra. It is now known that these are not even distinctive subspecies as they occur together in the same area and frequently inter-breed, producing both colours of kittens in a single litter.

Distribution of the jaguarundi (*Felis yagouaroundi*).

The precise relationships of this unusual cat are unclear. It is sometimes considered to be closely related to the puma, whereas others believe it is most similar to the flat-headed cat (see p. 112) from Asia. Unlike the vast majority of cats, however, the jaguarundi has no spots on its coat.

These cats may be encountered in a variety of habitats through their wide range, preferring lowland areas. They can live in relatively open countryside, but also in scrubland and forest. Jaguarundis may be found in swampy grassland and are able to swim well if necessary. They also tend to be more diurnal than many species, often hunting during the day. They prefer to hunt on the ground and will pursue a variety of creatures, depending to some extent on the locality. Small mammals feature prominently in their diet. The cat flattens its body as it moves in on its quarry, approaching as close as possible before striking. Birds may also be caught successfully, particularly if the cat can reach within 1.8 m (6 ft) of them, without being detected. Jaguarundis are said to eat fruit as well, but they do not usually enjoy it in captivity.

While its low height enables it to move easily through the undergrowth, the jaguarundi will also climb when needed. It has been suggested that they may rest off the ground in trees. These cats may sometimes be observed in pairs, although they normally appear to have a solitary lifestyle. In Paraguay, however, they might even share their territories with other pairs.

There appears to be no fixed breeding period, and kittens have been reported for much of the year from different areas. Females may have more than one litter in a year. As many as four offspring can be born about ten weeks after mating. The youngsters are blind at birth but have a coat of fur which, according to some reports, may be spotted. Their den may be a hollow tree, or simply a suitably concealed area under a bush. Jaguarundi kittens grow quite rapidly at first, and start to wander from the den when they are just a month old. Their mother will take them hunting, but abandons her kittens temporarily if disturbed. They are thought to be mature by their second year.

It is believed that the ancestors of this species crossed into North America from Asia via the land bridge in the company of the ancestral form of the puma. Today they are rare in the northern part of their range, although recently jaguarundis have become established in areas of Florida, the results of deliberate releases in the 1940s. Some of these could have been former pets.

The jaguarundi is said to tame well when obtained as a kitten. Natives in South America appear to have kept these cats quite frequently, well before the days of the sixteenth-century European invasion. They were kept as pets and to curb the rodent population around the villages. Jaguarundis have a relatively playful nature and can become tame, although they retain strong hunting instincts. When friendly they often purr and chirp, using a call not unlike that of a bird.

Jaguarundis are typically lazy hunters. They will take whatever prey is most readily available, with wild individuals proving bold by nature, to the extent of entering native villages after dark, and seizing poultry. They will try to creep close to the bird, keeping low in the grass or vegetation, before leaping at their quarry, grabbing the unfortunate bird around the neck, and dragging it off into cover. If pursued by dogs, jaguarundis will take to the trees, and are then capable of leaping from one branch to another, with considerable agility.

Geoffroy's cat *Felis geoffroyi*

DISTRIBUTION

Southern South America from the Bolivian Andes east and southwards to the mountainous region of north-western Argentina, also in parts of Uruguay, south-western Brazil and Paraguay. In Chile, this species may be found in the vicinity of the Straits of Magellan, making it (and the puma, which may also occur here) the most southerly distributed of all cats.

The name commemorates the French naturalist Geoffroy St Hilaire, who travelled widely in South America in the early 1800s.

Geoffroy's cat occurs in open woodland and scrubland, ranging from sea level up to 3500 m (11,500 ft) in the Bolivian Andes. It is known locally in Argentina as the *gato montes*, meaning 'mountain cat'. This species is one of a number of small, spotted cats found in this part of the world, and varies significantly in colour through its range. Resembling a domestic cat in size, Geoffroy's cat has a yellow ochre ground coloration in the northerly parts of its distribution, which changes to silvery grey in the south with considerable variation in between.

The black spots on the coat are prominent; those on the back and flanks are of roughly equal size. They tend to merge on the face to form stripes which extend over the forehead to the back of the neck. The ears are again covered with black fur, with a white spot at the centre of each. The tail, although spotted at its base,

Distribution of the Geoffroy's cat (*Felis geoffroyi*).

is ringed further down along its length. Melanistic individuals are not unknown, and there is also a variation in size between cats from different parts of their range. Those from the vicinity of Patagonia tend to be the largest, but in all cases males are bigger than females.

Originally it was thought that this species was closely related to the kodkod (see p. 134), but they are now considered to be separate. They have a number of features in common, however, not least the short, broad and convex shape of their skulls. The first pre-molar in each case is also remarkably small.

These cats are agile climbers, and spend much of their time in trees, where they are known to sleep in secure nooks. They may also hunt birds and small mammals in these surroundings, as well as on the ground. Geoffroy's cat is an adept swimmer, which may have enabled it to expand its range in the past, and it sometimes preys on fish.

This species is secretive by nature, and tends to stay away from human settlements. Their home range may be relatively small, varying from 2 to 3 sq km (0.8 to 1.2 sq miles) or so, depending partly on the availability of food. They are rarely seen, but are most likely to be observed crossing roads, either at first light or dusk, which suggests these cats are crepuscular in their habits.

At the present time Geoffroy's cat is one of the most common of the South American cats; it is considered to be much more numerous in Paraguay, for example, than the jaguarundi. Increasing development in certain parts of their range may well be having an adverse effect on their numbers, however. In the Paraguayan Chaco, for instances, cats may be vulnerable to traffic passing through this grassland area, as well as to direct disturbance.

In recent years Geoffroy's cats have also suffered increasing persecution from the skin trade as other species of spotted cat, such as the ocelot, become scarcer. This trend began in the late 1970s and in 1981 seventy thousand skins were imported to the Federal Republic of Germany alone. The majority originated from Paraguay and, to a lesser extent, Argentina. Steps have been taken within the European Community to regulate this trade effectively, and a ban on the import of skins was imposed in 1986.

One of the major problems concerning the trade is the need to ensure that, if it does take place, it is sustainable. This particular species was listed on CITES Appendix II, which would have permitted limited, non-detrimental trade. While the temporary closure of the European market made an impact on the numbers of skins being sold in the short term, there was always the risk that stock-piling would continue, waiting for trade here to recommence, and that new markets would open, and thus increase demand in the future. Locally in Paraguay, pelts are made into Indian headbands for tourists.

Fortunately now, following a decision taken at the CITES Conference of the Parties, held in Kyoto, Japan, during February 1992, this is far less likely to occur. The species was transferred to Appendix 1, protecting it from international trade. There was evidence that skins of protected species, such as the little spotted cat, were being misrepresented as those of Geoffrey's cat, while trade in skins of this species was continuing at an unsustainable level.

The breeding season of Geoffrey's cat is somewhat variable depending on area. It starts in the spring in the northern hemisphere, and kittens have been recorded from June to December. Females become especially vocal at this stage, often uttering a high-pitched wailing sound when they are in oestrus. This takes

Geoffroy's cat. Characterized by its broad head, this species also has tiny premolars. The black spots on the coat may be joined into stripes on occasions, and melanistic individuals have also been recorded.

place about every twenty-five days unless the female is pregnant. She will rub her head on objects in her territory, leaving her scent behind. Mating may sometimes take place in a tree.

The female soon starts to look for a den where she can give birth. It has been suggested that this may be off the ground, in a suitable tree hole, or alternatively it might be under a bush. Other sites, such as a rocky crevice, can also be chosen. Pregnancy lasts about ten weeks, after which two or three kittens form the typical litter. They develop quite rapidly, and are able to stand when only four days old. By six weeks of age the kittens are already agile climbers, and will be weaned about a month later. If she loses her litter, however, the female may mate again in less than two weeks, and it is possible that these small cats may produce two litters a year at least in some parts of their range.

Geoffroy's cat is solitary by nature, however, and males appear to play no part in the rearing of youngsters. The relatively small size of their home range means they may occur at relatively high densities, in areas of suitable habitat. The adaptability of their feeding habits means that obtaining suitable prey does not present serious obstacles in terms of their distribution.

Kodkod *Felis guigna*

DISTRIBUTION

Occurs in a restricted area on the south-western side of South America, in Chile and the Andean lake district of Argentina, where it is found in the provinces of Santa Cruz and Chubut.

Living in relatively open countryside, as well as in wooded and more densely forested regions, the kodkod is the smallest of the New World cats, weighing as little as 2.1 kg $(5\frac{1}{2}$ lb) when adult. It is also sometimes referred to as the guina. Relatively little is known about it, apart from the fact that there are two distinctive forms. The race which occurs in central Chile, *Felis guigna tigrillo*, is relatively plain in coloration, with no spots on its feet. It is larger than *Felis guigna guigna*, which lives in the southern part of the range, is more brightly coloured and has black spots extending to the feet.

The body coloration of the kodkod varies from buff to brownish grey, with dense black spots which sometimes merge to form streaks. Black rings encircle the tail, which has a black tip. Again, melanistic individuals have been recorded on occasions. The claws are relatively large, but the functional significance of their size is unclear; it may assist them in climbing.

Althought the kodkod was first documented and named in 1782 by a Jesuit priest called Juan Ignacio Molina who was resident in Santiago, virtually nothing has been recorded about its habits since then. The species is generally

Distribution of the kodkod (*Felis guigna*).

assumed to be rare, but is not threatened by the skin trade. It has been documented as being quite common in the area around Valdiva, however, but its numbers may be affected by deforestation in parts of its range.

The kodkod is thought to prey on small mammals, and has also been said to raid poultry houses, even sometimes in small groups. Its reproductive habits are unknown.

Ocelot *Felis pardalis*

DISTRIBUTION
Ranges from Arizona, south-western Texas and New Mexico southwards as far as Peru, Paraguay and northern Argentina.

It has been said that no two ocelots are identical, and this species is certainly a taxonomist's nightmare. The ground colour of these cats can range from pale yellow via reddish grey to pure grey. The markings extending along the back and sides are relatively elongated, rather than rounded, and have paler centres. The legs are typically spotted on the outer sides, with more evident blotching on their inner surfaces. There are white spots in the centre of the dark, rounded ears, and the entire underside of the body and legs is also whitish.

The range in markings may assist ocelots to conceal themselves in a variety of terrains. They tend to prefer countryside where there is plenty of cover, as they

Distribution of the ocelot (*Felis pardalis*).

135

The attractive markings of the ocelot (*Felis pardalis*) has meant that this species has been heavily hunted for its fur in the past.

are shy by nature and generally avoid human settlements, although they may occasionally take poultry and even young calves.

These relatively large cats may be seen during the daytime, although they may also rest in tree hollows at this time. They appear to hunt mainly on the ground, but can climb effectively when necessary. An interesting feature which sets them apart from most other cats is that ocelots usually live in pairs. If need be, they can also swim well.

Ocelots will use their pace to chase prey for short distances, taking deer, young peccaries, monkeys, agoutis and occasional reptiles such as snakes. Typically, they hunt in the early morning and at dusk. Small rodents may also feature in their diet, but the pair rarely hunt together or spend much time in each other's company in their territory. They keep in touch by their mewing calls and scent-marking however, which helps to reveal when the female is ready to mate.

Oestrus usually last for about five days. Kittens may be produced at any time of year, although in Paraguay mating tends to take place in October and November, occuring at night. The young are born in a well-concealed den approximately eleven weeks later, with the average litter consisting of just one or two kittens. The male ocelot helps to provide for his family, bringing food to the den. The coloration of the kittens at birth does not differ significantly from that of the adults. The weaning process begins at seven weeks old, but they may not breed for another two years.

The number of ocelots has been severely affected in many areas by hunting pressures: over 216,000 pelts were traded in the ten-year period ending in 1985. Many of these were exported from Paraguay, but a proportion are likely to have been smuggled across the border from Brazil where the species was protected. By the late 1970s there was little doubt that this species was declining badly, and trappers were unable to supply the demand for skins. This in turn led to the increasing exploitation of other small South American cats. Happily there are now signs that their numbers are starting to increase again after the transfer of all subspecies to CITES Appendix I, outlawing commercial trade in specimens taken from the wild. But it has been suggested that in some areas of Paraguay the decline in the numbers of ocelots has enabled Geoffroy's cats and jaguars to exploit this vacant ecological niche, and they have benefited at the expense of this species.

Little spotted cat *Felis tigrina*

DISTRIBUTION
Occurs through Central America from Costa Rica southwards as far as northern Argentina. It is not found in either Bolivia or Chile.

Also known as the oncilla or tiger cat, this species is small: even the largest males weigh no more than 2.8 kg (6 lb). The black spots are set against an ochre ground colour and may appear rather like blotches, which are noticeably smaller than in the margay (see p. 138). Facial stripes are also less apparent, and the underparts are whitish. The fur itself is thick, soft and short, with more definite black rings on the tail, which has a matching tip. It is not unusual for melanistic individuals

Distribution of the little spotted cat (*Felis tigrina*).

to be encountered: in some areas they can comprise 20 per cent of the population.

The little spotted cat favours wooded countryside and is an agile climber. It may be found in both humid lowland forest as well as montane cloud forest, where it ranges to an altitude of 1000 m (3300 ft). This species is thought to prey on a variety of small creatures, some of which may be caught off the ground, but its precise habits are something of a mystery.

Kittens tend to be born mainly between February and August. Studies involving captive little spotted cats have revealed that, after a gestation period lasting around eleven weeks, one or two offspring will be produced. Interestingly, it appears that all their teeth erupt at approximately the same stage, rather than gradually. In spite of being smaller than a domestic cat, the little spotted cat can be highly aggressive and has been known to kill its larger relative. On the rare occasions when hybridization between these two forms has occurred successfully, a high percentage of the resulting kittens have usually been born dead, because of the genetic mismatch.

Little spotted cats, too, have been hunted heavily for their fur in recent years; and the trade peaked once the ocelot and Geoffroy's cat had become scarce – a sad reflection on human greed. It climbed from around 13,000 a year in 1977 up to over 84,500 in 1983 according to CITES figures. The effects of this hunting pressure on the population, particularly in Paraguay which supplied most of the skins, are unclear, but it is believed that this species is not generally common in spite of having a wide range. Habitat loss is also of concern to the survival of these cats in some areas.

Margay *Felis wiedii*

Distribution
Extends over a wide area, from Mexico in Central America southwards to Argentina, east of the Andes.

These cats are very similar to the ocelot in terms of coloration and markings, but are significantly smaller. They can also be distinguished easily by their tail, which is much longer, reflecting the margay's tree-climbing habits. This has given rise to its alternative common name – long-tailed spotted cat. Margays also have a short, rounded head and larger eyes, which may indicate a nocturnal lifestyle – although in fact these cats tend to be active during the day.

They may rely heavily on vision as they move through the treetops. It has been suggested that these cats are even capable of running beneath branches, gripping on with their sharp claws. Certainly there can be no doubt that margays are specialized for an arboreal lifestyle; unlike all other cats they can run head-first down a tree to the ground, rather than moving down backwards.

This species is found in a variety of wooded habitats: those occuring in mountainous areas tend to have more prominent black markings than margays found in stretches of lowland forest. In some regions margays have invaded both cocoa and coffee plantations, which suggests that they can be adaptable. Their new choice of habitat might actually help their survival, if they are able to dispatch rodents which might otherwise harm these crops.

Distribution of the margay (*Felis wiedii*).

Little is known about their hunting habits, although most of their prey is probably obtained off the ground. Monkeys, birds, tree frogs and lizards are all taken by these cats. It is believed that margays live solitary lives, communicating through a series of calls which range from notes of greeting to aggressive warnings.

When the female comes into oestrus, which can be at virtually any time of the year (although there may be regional variations), she scent-marks branches by rubbing her head over them. The male approaches cautiously, usually smelling her ano-genital area before mating takes place, often in trees. It is a brief encounter. About twelve weeks later the female may well give birth to what is usually a solitary kitten in a tree hollow. The kitten has black spots and grey paws at this stage, and emerges outside the nest for the first time around five weeks of age. Males are significantly bigger than females, and may take longer to mature as a consequence.

The skins of these cats too have been heavily traded in the past, and figures suggested a declining population, certainly in the southern part of their range, from the late 1970s to the mid-1980s when legal trade ceased. Deforestation now represents an even more serious threat to the future of these cats in many parts of their range. Nowhere are they thought to occur in high numbers. The margay may have formerly ranged into the USA, where it is known from a single specimen and certainly now its population has fallen dramatically, as far as can be ascertained, throughout Central America.

Pampas cat *Felis colocolo*

DISTRIBUTION
Ranges from Ecuador and Peru southwards to Brazil, Paraguay, Bolivia, Chile, Argentina and Patagonia.

Bearing a striking resemblance to the wild cat of Europe, the pampas cat is characterized by its relatively broad face and pointed ears. In noticeable contrast to most of the smaller New World cats, its coat is not spotted with black. Instead it is basically silvery grey in colour, with reddish brown bands running over the body. These stripes, which are especially apparent on the legs, may sometimes be broken into spots. Individuals vary quite widely however, with some being more heavily patterned than others. The fur in all cases is long, and may form a mane running down the back. This can measure up to 7 cm ($2\frac{1}{2}$ in) long, and the hairs are held erect if the cat is frightened, giving it a rather ferocious appearance. The tail too is quite bushy.

There are noticeable regional differences in coloration: pampas cats from the north of the range have greyish backs to their ears, with central white spots, while those from the south are simply grey. In addition, the barring running from the corners of the eyes to the ears is more pronounced in cats from western areas. Melanistic variants have also been documented.

Distribution of the pampas cat (*Felis colocolo*).

The scientific name of this species, *Felis colocolo*, probably commemorates Colocolo, a noted Araucanian warrior chief who was known to Juan Molina who was the librarian at the Jesuit College in Santiago, Chile. He chose this name when he originally documented the cat in 1782, but subsequently the species was divided, with the population south of Buenos Aires in Argentina being described as *Felis pajeros* in accordance with the local name of *gato pajero*, meaning 'grass cat'. This distinction no longer applies, although seven different races are now recognized.

In spite of its name, the pampas cat is not found just in areas of grassland. It occurs in humid forested areas in Salta and Tucuman provinces in Argentina, for example, and also lives at relatively high altitudes.

The species is not found in coastal areas, but may occur even in fairly densely populated regions of Chile.

Pampas cats appear to spend most of their time on the ground, hunting small animals such as guinea pigs and ground-dwelling birds, notably tinamous. They probably tend not to ambush prey, but simply pursue it. Domestic poultry may sometimes fall victim to these cats.

The breeding period appears to be restricted, at least in captivity, to the months between April and July. A female killed in the wild was also found to be pregnant in April. Details about the cat's breeding habits are otherwise unknown. Litter size appears to be small, however, and may consist of just a single kitten.

The status of the pampas cat is also something of a mystery. From 1976 to 1979 more than 78,000 skins of this species, with an estimated value of 1.8 million US dollars, were exported via Buenos Aries, but prior to this there was apparently little trade in their fur. Since 1980 the number of pelts being traded dropped dramatically, largely as the result of legal protection in Argentina.

It is believed that these cats are relatively rare in many parts of their range, but they may be locally common in some areas. Unlike some of the other smaller felids they are reputedly aggressive, and not responsive to taming.

Andean mountain cat *Felis jacobita*

DISTRIBUTION
Occurs in the Andes of southern Peru, Bolivia, north-eastern Chile and northern Argentina.

The coloration of this species is not unlike that of the pampas cat. It is pale silvery grey, becoming more ashy over the back and paler, bordering on white, on the underparts. Spots occur in diagonal lines, blackish beneath, on the legs and belly, but becoming brown and even orangish yellow across the back. The coat itself has a distinctly fine, soft texture: individual hairs are about 4 cm (2 in) on the back and get shorter over the tail. This has a light tip, and is typically marked with nine blackish or brown rings. The ears are dark grey.

In terms of overall appearance, too, the Andean mountain cat is not dissimilar to the pampas cat. Its skull structure is unique, however, in that it has a double-chambered bulla, which in the past led to it being classified separately as *Oreailurus jacobita*.

Distribution of the Andean mountain cat (*Felis jacobita*).

This cat occurs at high altitudes in the Andean region, where it is generally found above 3000 m (10,000 ft). It is known to range up to 5100 m (16,730 ft) in Peru, but remains one of the least known of all the South American cats. It is said to be found above the snow line in some cases, and inhabits rocky, treeless terrain where rainfall is low and the weather is invariably windy and cold. Here, the Andean mountain cat preys on viscachas and chinchillas, as well as other rodents, but nothing else appears to be documented about its habits. The species is generally considered rare.

Puma *Felis concolor*

DISTRIBUTION
Extends from Canada southwards, being found west of the Great Plains and down to southern Florida, through Mexico and Central America, and extending across most of South America.

Although the puma is still the most widely distributed of the New World's wild cats, its range has constricted dramatically in recent years, particularly in North America, where it is now confined largely to the western side of the continent. It is known under a wide range of local names, including cougar, panther, mountain devil, Mexican lion and mountain lion, in spite of the fact that these cats are not related. The puma purrs, in the way of members of the genus *Felis*, and has a similar scream rather than a roar, although it differs from its generic relatives in that its pupils constrict to a circular opening rather than a vertical slit.

The size and coloration of the puma vary noticeably through its huge area of distribution, with males usually being heavier than their mates, weighing up to 103 kg (227 lb). Those originating from temperate regions are larger than pumas found in the tropical zone, because for part of the year they have more food available and therefore grow more rapidly. This concept is now more generally accepted than the older theory that animals in temperate areas grew larger because this gave them a lower body surface area to volume ratio, which meant that they lost less heat from their bodies.

As a general guide, the puma's coloration ranges from shades of red and brown to grey, sometimes bordering on silver. In common with the African lion, the puma has no markings on its coat. In arid areas the species is most likely to be brown, with red pumas tending to predominate in tropical areas. Grey pumas are most likely to be seen in the north of their range, but there is considerable variation. As an example, American President Theodore Roosevelt shot both red and slate-grey pumas in Colorado. Melanism is know to occur only in the populations of Central and South America. Albino pumas are even rarer. Coat length also varies somewhat, depending on the area of distribution. It is shorter in the tropical areas, and longer, with a softer, less bristly texture elsewhere.

Distribution of the puma (*Felis concolor*).

Pumas are highly adaptable in habitat and can be found from sea level up to altitudes of 4500 m (15,000 ft). They can occur in swampland and are able to swim well if necessary, although they avoid water if possible. Tropical and coniferous forest may also be home to them, as can open grassland and stretches of semi-desert.

These cats have a great ability to merge into their background, in spite of their relatively large size. Pumas are shy, wary and elusive, and predominantly nocturnal in their habits, especially in areas where they may encounter people. They can run at speed when necessary – if they are being pursued by dogs, for example – and can also use their powerful hindquarters to jump considerable distances, approaching 12 m (about 40 ft).

Their prey varies according to area, although deer are taken throughout their range. Pumas tend to hunt by stalking, using whatever natural cover is available, before striking, often by leaping on to the animal. The resulting impact may be sufficient to kill the prey; if not, the puma will dispatch it with a bite. In South America pumas have even been observed hunting monkeys in the trees, chasing them from one tree to another by jumping from branch to branch. In spite of their pace, pumas are not equipped for a sustained chase. If they lose the initiative, and are not able to seize their prey almost immediately, they will give up and look elsewhere.

When they make a kill, these cats drag it away some distance, up to 400 m (1300 ft), to some sheltered place where they are less likely to be disturbed. Pumas are able to pull animals much heavier than themselves: one is known to have moved a 250 kg (560 lb) heifer out of a waterhole and hauled it part of the way up a mountainside.

The viscera may be devoured first, or the meat in the vicinity of the thigh. Having eaten, the puma will often cover the remains of its kill with vegetation and may then return to feed later, possibly over the course of a week if it does not make another kill during this period. After feeding the puma is likely to return to its den and rest.

Pumas can be quite prolific, producing up to six offspring in a litter. The female rears the young on her own, and they start hunting with her when they are six months old. Then, just over a year later, she will drive them off, and they may wander over 100 km (60 miles or so), before they can establish new territories.

Although the puma is not considered to be generally aggressive towards people, the number of attacks appears to be on the increase with more being reported in recent years. In some instances this is because the puma is suffering from rabies, which causes it to become overtly aggressive. There was a sad case of two boys being attacked by a puma close to Morgan Hill, California. A woman who helped them was also injured and died of rabies, along with one of the boys, seven weeks later.

The risk of attacks is relatively slight, however. There have been only fifty documented attacks across North America in the past century, resulting in nine fatalities. The majority of these occured in British Columbia, nineteen of them on Vancouver Island. Children are most at risk, but pumas are easily deterred from persisting if the victim fights back. They are most likely to attack when someone is bending down, since in this position the person is most likely to resemble their usual prey. The cat tends to circle the person beforehand, crouching down and

Although pumas (*Felis concolor*) are confined to the New World, there have been persistent reports of pumas at large in Britain, which presumably must have escaped here or been released. The most famous of these is the so-called Surrey puma, named after the county where many sightings were made in the mid-1970s.

sometimes screaming or yowling. Throwing an object such as a shoe at the puma is the most successful means of deterring an attack.

Pumas are now being seen more in urban areas of North America, and are becoming bolder. John Seidensticker, an authority on the puma and other large cats, has suggested that this is because in many regions pumas are now the dominant carnivores. If both bears and wolves are eliminated, pumas fill this niche. Increasing development of towns and cities is also taking place, which brings pumas into closer contact with people. In the case of Vancouver, the ideal puma habitat is just 8 km (5 miles) from the city centre. Young cats, once they are independent, are being pushed out into the suburbs from here by older, established individuals. As they are not hunted in the suburbs their numbers increase and they are less fearful and consequently more of a menace.

There is no doubt that human pressures have exerted a toll on puma numbers in various parts of North America, however. As a result the eastern panther (*Felis concolor cougar*) has been brought to the verge of extinction – if it is not, as some people believe, already extinct. This race of puma formerly extended from the eastern USA into Canada, and westwards to Alberta and the edge of the Great Plains.

In spite of the fact that it was certainly very scarce even by the early 1900s, odd eastern panthers were still being shot in a number of eastern states on rare occasions. There have been persistent sightings as well. Finally, the shooting of a puma during 1971 north of Crossville in eastern Tennessee led the US Department of the Interior to revise the status of the eastern panther, listing it as endangered rather than extinct. Most recent reports of sightings, according to the Eastern Puma Research Network, have been made in West Virginia.

A photograph has also been taken in Chaplin, Connecticut, of what appeared to be a young puma. There is some dispute, however, as to whether these sightings refer to genuine eastern panthers or to escaped or discarded pets. At the present time twelve states in the USA allow pumas to be harvested, and it is estimated that over fifty are taken annually for rearing as pets. Since pumas may live for up to twenty years, this means that their captive population may be numbering many hundreds, if not thousands. What is not in doubt, however, is that the secretive and adaptable nature of these cats suggests that eliminating them from such a vast area of territory would be a major undertaking, even if such a policy were to be carried out with dedicated commitment. On balance, therefore, the probability is that they do still survive, albeit in very reduced numbers.

Further south in the USA, the status of the Florida race of the puma (*Felis concolor coryi*) has become critical, although there is no doubt that this population still exists. Numbering between thirty and fifty individuals according to the latest estimates, these cats have declined in the face of greatly increased development in the area, after decades of hunting pressure. This race used to be widely distributed through the southern states, from eastern Texas through Arkansas and Mississippi into parts of Tennessee, South Carolina and Florida.

Attempts to save it began in 1976, with the setting up of a Recovery Team appointed by the US Fish and Wildlife Service. Their plan was approved in 1981, and subsequently revised six years later. Considerable effort has been put into maintaining a secure area of habitat for these cats. Already 891 million hectares (3.4 million sq miles) is in public ownership, and further acquisitions are planned.

Radio-tracking of the remaining Florida panthers has provided information about their movements and where they cross roads. Collisions with vehicles represent the greatest direct threat to these cats – between 1972 and 1991 seventeen died as a result. The Federal Government has included special underpasses in the building of Interstate 75, with thirty-six crossing points, backed by fences to prevent the pumas wandering across the road itself.

Health monitoring of the remaining population has also been carried out by the Florida Fish and Game Commission. The females in particular were in a generally poor state of health which was thought to be slowing their rate of reproduction, although today it is believed that the population is no longer declining in numbers.

As well as heavy infestations of parasites, antibodies to both feline panleuco-paenia virus and feline calici virus were detected in the majority of the fourteen Florida panthers tested. Both can be fatal, and feline panleucopaenia is especially serious during pregnancy, infecting unborn kittens and causing permanent damage to their nervous systems. This may well have affected their numbers in the past although with antibodies present, their offspring will now benefit from maternal immunity. Bobcats from the same area also showed similar high evidence of past infections, which could possibly be linked to the domestic cat population here.

Mercury levels in some parts of their habitat are thought to have been a contributory factor in the death of two Florida panthers. Even more worrying has been the very high incidence of abnormal spermatazoa obtained from males of this race – 93 per cent of the samples were affected . This could undoubtedly be having an effect on the conception rate of those females capable of breeding.

As a result of these serious problems faced by the remaining individuals in the wild, a captive breeding programme has been established. It has begun with a pair of cats which had been injured in road accidents, along with six kittens obtained in 1991. Considerable publicity has also been given to the plight of the Florida panther in its last remaining stronghold, and this cat was designated the official mammal of the state in 1982.

SUBFAMILY PANTHERINAE

The members of this subfamily include the large cats, as well as the lynx. In a number of cases hybridization has confirmed the close relationships between these cats, although this does not appear to take place in the wild, where their distributions are likely to overlap. It has proved possible to produce both ligers, from the crossing of a male lion with a tigress, and tigrons, from the reverse pairing. In most cases such hybrid offspring are infertile, but a liger at Munich Zoo produced a cub when paired with a lion. An even more bizarre series of matings took place at Chicago Zoo, where the cubs resulting from a jaguar × leopard pairing were then bred successfully with a lion.

Caracal *Lynx caracal*

DISTRIBUTION
Occurs over a wide area of Africa although it is absent from parts of the south as well as rainforest and the Saharan region. Extends across the Arabian peninsula, although again absent from desert areas, into Asia, extending via Iran and Afghanistan to central India.

This species bears a striking resemblance to the lynx, although the subject of their relationship is a matter of dispute. The caracal is sometimes classified on its own, in a genus of this name.

Smaller in overall size than the lynx, it is reddish brown with whitish areas on the chin and throat as well as on the underparts. White hair surrounds the eyes, but there are no spots on the coat. The distinctive ears are narrow and pointed, with prominent black tufts of hair at their tips which may be 5 cm (2 in) long. Melanistic caracals have been reported only from Africa, although there is no reason to assume that they may not occur elsewhere in the species' range. There is usually noticeable sexual dimorphism in a population, with males being larger than females and weighing up to 20 kg (44 lb).

These cats are found in relatively arid countryside, rather than true desert, in spite of sometimes being called the desert lynx. They are solitary by nature, and although they may be encountered during the day, they are more likely to be active at night.

Caracals are very agile, and adept at jumping to catch birds. These are knocked down with the cat's paws, and this behaviour gave rise to the expression, 'putting the cat among the pigeons'. In India, tame caracals were placed in

Caracal (*Lynx caracal*): the name of this cat describes the coloration of its ears, originating from the Turkish word *karakal*, which translates as 'black-eared'.

a ring with a group of these birds, and bets were made on the number which would be knocked down at a single strike. They have also been trained for hunting purposes, rather like dogs, to pursue hares, birds and other small game.

These cats will catch a wide variety of prey. A recent study carried out in Israel revealed that mammals were the major food item here, comprising nearly two-thirds of their diet. This included both Egyptian mongooses (*Herpestes ichneumon*) and desert hedgehogs (*Paraechinus aethiopicus*). Birds were also taken quite regularly, along with *Uromastyx* lizards and other reptiles, as well as some insects. Vegetable matter formed part of their diet too.

Caracals may attack domestic stock, and frequently kill relentlessly under such circumstances. In Cape Province, South Africa, caracals were found to engage in surplus killing more frequently than leopards. On one occasion twenty-one young goats were slaughtered by a single caracal but only one of the carcasses was eaten.

Male caracals have a range which may be four times larger in area than that of females, and they also cover a greater distance. The reason may be to locate

Distribution of the caracal (*Lynx caracal*).

females coming into oestrus, since there is no set breeding period in this species. A number of males will be drawn to the area, and each will mate in turn with the female. The oldest and largest males are dominant at this stage.

Mating occurs at intervals of about forty-eight hours on average, and during this period the female may have three separate partners. Two cubs appear to form the average litter, with the female giving birth in a disused burrow or a crevice in the rocks after a gestation period of around eleven weeks. The family start to move by the time the youngsters are about a month old, changing their location each day and hiding in thick vegetation. Independent by six months old, the young caracals will leave their mother's territory about four months later. They may move 90 km (56 miles) or more to establish their own home ranges, which can still overlap with that of the adult female. In Asia particularly, caracals have now declined quite seriously in numbers, to the point that all the races here are considered to be endangered.

In spite of their relatively small size, caracals are powerful wild cats, and quite able to take prey much larger than themselves, such as impala (*Aepyceros melampus*). Their agility helps them to inflict a fatal blow before their larger opponent has an opportunity to escape. They are generally quiet by nature, but do possess a call similar to that of a leopard. Their unusual name is derived from the Turkish word 'karakal', which means 'black ears', and refers to the coloration of the fur present on the back of their ears, and the distinctive tufts here as well. Its longer tail serves to distinguish the caracal from the true lynxes.

Spanish lynx *Lynx pardinus*

DISTRIBUTION
Confined to the south-west of Spain and restricted localities in Portugal.

The Spanish lynx is similar in general appearance to the Eurasian lynx, and is sometimes classified as a subspecies rather than as a species in its own right. It can be distinguished quite easily, however, by its heavily spotted coat and smaller size. Even the males do not exceed 13 kg (29 lb), which is only about half the weight of the Eurasian lynx.

The range of the Spanish lynx has been greatly reduced in recent years. It is confined to the wooded parts of remote mountainous regions and to the scrub and sand dunes of the Coto Doñana. Here the Doñana National Park remains the last major stronghold of the Spanish lynx. During the 1960s, its numbers were estimated at a maximum of two hundred, of which up to 10 per cent were being killed legally each year. The Spanish lynx used to range widely over the Iberian peninsula, but hunting pressure has led to a dramatic fall in its numbers. The relatively few survivors are also being killed in leg traps intended to catch rabbits, and run over on the roads.

The Spanish lynx is predominantly nocturnal and solitary by nature. Hares and rabbits are its main diet, but it may also prey on fallow deer fawns, ducks and fish amongst other items. It can swim well, and is sufficiently agile to knock red-legged partridges (*Alectoris rufa*) out of the air, having flushed them from the ground. A neck bite is typically used to dispatch larger quarry.

The fall in the numbers of lynxes has now had serious effects on the ecosystem within the Doñana National Park, according to a recent study here. There has been a correspondingly dramatic increase in the red fox (*Vulpes vulpes*) population. In the past, lynxes restricted the numbers of foxes here by directly competing for food. Both lynxes and foxes depended upon the supply of rabbits for food. When the rabbits are scarce, as in 1982, few if any young lynxes managed to survive. The foxes thrived as they were more easily able to adapt their eating

Distribution of
the Spanish lynx
(*Lynx pardinus*).

habits to other available sources of food. Over time, the more opportunistic fox would increase in numbers as the lynx became scarcer. Subsequently, once the rabbit population began to increase again, it would be harder for the lynxes to re-establish themselves because of the increased number of foxes already resident in the area. Lynxes are not especially adaptable in their feeding habits in any event. The serious drought which affected the region from 1979 to 1983 undoubtedly reduced rabbit numbers, and the situation was compounded by an outbreak of myxomatosis. It may well be necessary to curb the number of foxes in order to assist the recovery of the lynx population.

The breeding habits of the Spanish lynx are unusual in that males appear to move to new areas where they are joined by females; this is the reverse of the situation in other felids, as far as is known. Mating usually occurs in January, followed by a gestation period of just over nine weeks. The young are weaned at about five months old, and separate from their mother just before the next breeding season. It may take three years before they themselves breed for the first time. The total world population of Spanish lynx is currently estimated to be four hundred at most.

Eurasian lynx *Lynx lynx*

DISTRIBUTION

Extends from parts of western Europe, including Scandinavia, eastwards through the former USSR to Mongolia and Manchuria, and is widely distributed in northern and central parts of Asia. Also present in Iran, Iraq and Asia Minor.

There is again considerable dispute as to whether the Eurasian lynx should simply be known as the lynx, incorporating the Canadian lynx into this grouping as the subspecies *Lynx lynx canadensis*. However, the Eurasian lynx is about twice as large as its North American counterpart and usually more strikingly marked, with clearly defined black spots on a yellowish brown ground colour.

Seasonal changes are also apparent, with the spotting being less evident during the winter months when the coat is longer. In addition, those lynxes from the northern part of their range tend to have less distinctive markings than those occurring further south. There is normally a ruff of longer hair encircling the neck. The feet are large and well protected by fur, which enables them to walk over frozen ground.

The lynx is most likely to be found in forest regions, where there is plenty of cover available. It may also be seen in scrubland and relatively rocky terrain.

Not surprisingly, the increasing urbanization of western Europe and loss of forested areas has led to a severe reduction in the lynx population. Even in some regions of Asia their numbers are likely to be adversely affected. The sighting of a lynx in St Petersburg early in 1989 confirmed that these cats are now being encountered closer to major towns and cities. In this instance, after three days the animal was successfully captured and taken to a forest area well away from the city.

A meeting of specialists was held at Neuchâtel in Switzerland during October 1980 to discuss the worrying status of the lynx in Europe. As a relatively large

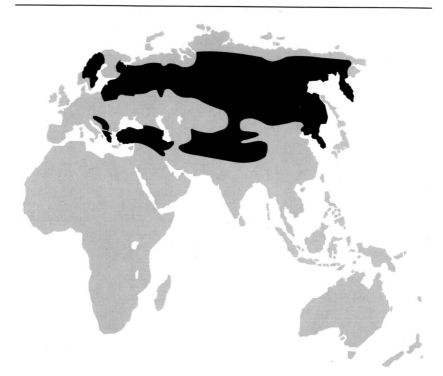

Distribution of the Eurasian lynx (*Lynx lynx*).

predatory species, the lynx poses particular problems when reintroduction schemes are tried out. Only three out of nine attempts made since then appear to have achieved any lasting success. Two of these schemes were organized in the Swiss catons of Jura and Obwalden, where about twenty lynxes from the Carpathian Mountains were released. Since then, it is estimated that they have spread to occupy about two-thirds of the available territory in the Swiss Alps. Here it has been shown by radio-tracking that lynxes require vast territories: those occupied by a male range from 200 to 400 sq km (about 80–150 sq miles), while those of females extend over an area of 100 to 150 sq km (about 40–60 sq miles) and typically overlap with that of a male.

The total lynx population in Switzerland is now estimated to be between fifty and one hundred, but not everyone is pleased at the return of this predatory species. Studies have shown that approximately 85 per cent of the lynx's diet in this region comprises chamois and roe deer, as well as red deer fawns and smaller mammals; each lynx makes between fifty and eighty kills of this type annually. But unfortunately they also occasionally prey on farmstock. Between 1973 and 1979 losses of domestic stock attributed to lynxes, for which compensation was paid, were 533 animals; the annual figure is now about fifty, the majority of which are sheep.

This has led to calls to curb the lynx population, especially in the canton of Valais. Farmers have attacked the compensation scheme on the basis that it does not provide for indirect losses resulting from stress caused to the animals. Hunters too have criticized the reintroduction programme, expressing concern that it will hamper attempts to save various other species such as the capercaillie (*Tetrao urogallus*) from extinction in Switzerland.

The evidence suggests, however, that such concerns are misplaced. A three-year study carried out within an area containing seven hundred roe deer, a similar number of chamois and a pair of lynxes showed that the cats killed just 100 animals. In contrast 278 others were found dead from other causes, while hunters accounted for a further 490.

Elsewhere in Europe, lynxes are again being hunted. In Finland, where the population has grown from virtually zero in the 1950s to over five hundred, thirty years later, special hunting licences began to be issued in 1968. in Häme, one of the areas where they are now common, the lynx preys mainly on North American white-tailed deer (*Odocoileus virginianus*), which were introduced here over fifty years ago. Hares are equally significant in their diet here, in an area where roe deer are very scarce.

The recolonization of Finland occurred naturally, with lynxes moving here from neighbouring Scandinavian countries and the former USSR. It is now thought that the numbers of lynxes in Sweden are currently between two and

The Eurasian lynx (*Lynx lynx*) can be distinguished from its Canadian relative by its larger size, while its black markings are also usually more distinctive. These lynxes prefer forested areas, where there is good cover available for them.

three hundred, and there is clear evidence that the population has fallen here in recent years. This is believed to be due not only to excessive hunting pressure, but also to feline panleucopaenia virus and sarcoptic mange. However the species has been fully protected since 1986, with Lapps in reindeer areas receiving compensation for attacks by lynxes. Reindeer are a major item of the lynx's diet in northern Sweden, and over 70 per cent of attacks result in a successful kill. This may be linked to the fact that reindeer do not differentiate between lynxes and herding dogs, making them easy prey.

On the most recent figures, the lynx population across the former USSR, where the species has traditionally been valued for its fur, is estimated to be between 36,000 and 40,000. Declines in some areas have been noticed; the species has disappeared from Moldavia, just north of the Black Sea, for example. Lynx populations also appear to have shifted to other areas, moving into Kamchatka in eastern Siberia in the 1930s, and elsewhere in tundra, steppe and forested regions. Lynx hunting is regulated, and in some areas is banned.

The lynx population which survived in the Czechoslovakian Carpathians has undergone a rapid increase in numbers since the end of the Second World War. Estimates of their population here vary from five hundred to nine hundred, and in northern Moravia and Sumava regulation through hunting has become necessary.

The situation is less satisfactory in Poland, where there may be fewer than two hundred still surviving, and poaching remains a problem. Hunting bans can be very effective at allowing the recovery of lynx numbers however, as has been demonstrated in Turkey. Here, lynxes are fully protected in reserves covering 15,000 sq km (5800 sq miles) and strict controls have been imposed on killing lynx elsewhere in the country.

In the former Yugoslavia, the release of three pairs of lynxes in the Medved hunting preserve in Slovenia during March 1973 has enabled regulated hunting to be resumed, as the population here has grown. According to the latest estimates, lynxes now occupy an area of some 6000 sq km (2300 sq miles) in Croatia and Slovenia.

In France there are also signs of an increase in the lynx population. Individuals from the Jura release project in Switzerland have now crossed into France and started to re-establish themselves here as well. A separate release scheme has been carried out in Alsace, in the Vosges Mountains, and there is clear evidence that a population still survives in the French Pyrenees, in spite of the fact that the last individual was thought to have been shot in 1957.

Clearly, if hunting pressures can be lifted in areas of suitable habitat lynx populations are capable of regeneration. Where reintroduction schemes are attempted large tracts of territory are essential. The support of the local people is another vital component in ensuring their success – as the Swiss experience confirms, there may be considerable prejudice against such endeavours, resulting in the killing of the introduced animals. One of the four lynxes involved in the Vosges project, who by this stage had three cubs, was shot within a year of her release. Even so, other releases are likely, notably in Italy.

It is typically a rather slow process building up numbers in the wild, because females are unlikely to produce more than two or three offspring in a litter, and breed only once a year, although on occasions, four or five cubs may be born. Their maximum lifespan in the wild is thought to be around 13 years.

North American lynx *Lynx canadensis*

DISTRIBUTION

Occurs from Alaska right across Canada to Newfoundland. On the western side of its range it occurs down to northern California.

Similar in appearance to its Eurasian relative, but significantly smaller, with males weighing up to 10 kg (22 lb), the North American or Canadian lynx has a long coat. It also has large feet, which can be up to 10 cm (4 in) in diameter and are heavily furred to enable it to hunt effectively in snow. The tips of the ears are again covered with tufts of black hair, and the short tail ends in a black tip. The coat itself is often tipped with white, which gives the animal a frosted appearance.

The lifestyle of these cats is similar to that of the Eurasian lynx. They are solitary, although females are believed to hunt together occasionally when they have cubs. They possess very keen eyesight, which enables them to detect prey from a distance, and may also hunt by scent.

In North America, the numbers of lynxes are very closely related to that of their major prey, the snowshoe hare. When food is in short supply, their reproductive success falls dramatically, with a reduction in the conception rate and heavy mortality among the cubs. The peaks and troughs occur at intervals of about 9.6 years, with the snowshoe hare population falling before that of the lynx, as a result of disease, and then recovering first.

Distribution of the North American lynx (*Lynx canadensis*).

Prominent whiskers and ear tufts help to characterize the Canadian lynx (*Lynx canadensis*) which also has a longer, denser coat during the cold, winter months. Its feet are well covered with fur, which assists it when walking on snow.

It is surprising that the lynx does not simply hunt other creatures which remain numerous when the hares are scarce. They do feed on small rodents, ptarmigan and red deer, for example, but on the mainland they appear to have adapted to be almost totally dependent on the snowshoe hare. On Newfoundland in contrast, caribou fawns make up much of their diet. Having made a kill, however, the lynx may relinquish it if a wolverine appears, preferring not to risk an encounter with this determined member of the weasel family.

In North America, the lynx has long been hunted for its fur. Indeed, it was the returns of the Hudson Bay Company which first indicated the population cycle associated with this species. Skins were exceedingly scarce in some years and very numerous in others, which proved to be a recurring pattern.

As in Europe, the lynx has been driven out of parts of its range by hunting pressures and development. Yet at times, when population is peaking, some may move across the Canadian border into American states such as Minnesota and North Dakota. The lynx is also said to occur on a regular basis in Utah and New England, and may occasionally be seen elsewhere in the USA.

Bobcat *Lynx rufus*

Distribution
Ranges from the southern region of the Canadian provinces throughout all states in the USA down into southern Mexico.

Distribution of the bobcat (*Lynx rufus*).

157

Although resembling the North American lynx, this species can be recognized by its shorter legs and difference in coloration, which has led to it being known as the bay lynx in some parts of its range. Its ground colour may vary from shades of reddish brown through to light grey, with white underparts. Dark brown or black spots are present on the coat, and the fur on the ears in black, with white spots in the centre. The tufting at the tips is less prominent than in the lynx – some bobcats have no tufts.

Smaller and more adaptable by nature, the bobcat is found in a wide variety of habitats from semi-desert to sub-tropical swamp and coniferous forest. It is most likely to be encountered at altitudes below 1800 m (5900 ft), and does not appear to range above 3700 m (12,100 ft). Bobcats may remain relatively close to human settlements, hunting cautiously at night. The territory of a male typically encompasses that of several females, and may extend over an area of 175 sq km (67 sq miles).

Small mammals make up the bulk of the bobcat's diet. Hares and rabbits are frequently taken, along with various rodents and birds. Deer tend to be eaten in the winter, when bobcats frequently scavenge on their carcasses rather than actually kill them. Stealth rather than speed is used by the bobcat when hunting. This is why in New Mexico, for example, they prefer to prey on cotton-tailed rabbits rather than the faster and more common jack rabbits.

The relative small size of the bobcat leaves it vulnerable to attacks by other, larger cats which occur in parts of its range, notably jaguars and pumas. Even deer may attack bobcats on occasions: females are particularly aggressive in defence of their offspring.

The bobcat's relatively small size has meant that it is vulnerable to other wild cats, such as lynx, in its area of distribution.

The breeding season tends to peak between February and June. Courtship is a noisy affair, as the calls of the cats echo over a considerable distance at night. Up to six cubs may be born after a gestation period lasting about eight weeks. Both parents may subsequently provide food for them, and the young will venture forth from their den for the first time when they are about five weeks of age.

The young bobcats will start hunting with their mother from the age of five months. By the time they are nine months old they are starting to separate, in some cases wandering over 150 km (100 miles) before establishing their own territory. In many places bobcats remain relatively numerous, although they have declined in some eastern parts of the USA in particular.

Marbled cat *Pardofelis marmorata*

DISTRIBUTION
Southern Asia, extending from northern India and Nepal east via Burma to Thailand, Malaysia, Sumatra and Borneo.

Similar in appearance to the clouded leopard, but significantly smaller, the marbled cat is nevertheless closely related to the big cats. It grows to an apparent maximum total length of approximately 100 cm (40 in), of which its long tail contributes 40 cm (16 in).

The fur of these forest-dwelling cats is very soft in texture, with variable ground coloration. This can range from reddish brown through yellow to brownish grey, with a variety of dark markings in the form of blotches, spots and stripes. Marbled cats are highly arboreal by nature and probably hunt birds in the trees, although they may also catch rats and other creatures on the ground.

Believed to be mainly nocturnal in its habits, relatively little has been recorded about the marbled cat. It is reputed to be aggressive by nature, and usually has an arched posture even when standing. The breeding behaviour of this species in

Distribution of the marbled cat (*Pardofelis marmorata*).

The marbled cat (*Pardofelis marmorata*), though small in size, shows a close similarity to the clouded leopard in appearance.

the wild is not documented, but observations with captive marbled cats suggest there is no fixed breeding period. Pregnancy lasts just over eleven weeks, after which up to four youngsters are born. They are mottled at this stage, only starting to acquire the characteristic marbling on their coats from about six and a half weeks. Their pattern of markings is fully apparent by the time they are four months old.

The marbled cat is thought to be scarce throughout its range, and with widespread deforestation occurring in many areas here, there is particular concern for its future. The size of this species may have reduced to enable it to opt for an increasingly tree-based existence. In genetic terms it shows a close relationship with the tiger, and as such is one of the most enigmatic members of the entire cat family.

Clouded leopard *Neofelis nebulosa*

DISTRIBUTION
South-east Asia, from Nepal eastwards to southern China and Taiwan, and south to Malaysia, Borneo and Sumatra.

These cats are named after their cloud-like pattern of markings, which have blackish edges and paler centres. Their ground coloration varies from yellowish to grey, with black spots on the head, legs and tail. Stripes extend across the cheeks. Clouded leopards have a long body relative to their height, and show a number of anatomical peculiarities. The canine teeth are particularly large and narrow. Their eyes have the slit-like pupils characteristic of the small cats, rather than round ones, whereas the ossification of the hyoid arch suggests a closer affinity with the big cats.

Shy by nature and largely nocturnal, especially close to human settlements, these cats are found primarily in dense evergreen forests. Studying their habits is difficult. Indeed, there was no confirmed occurrence of the species in Nepal between 1863 and 1987, aside from several sightings recorded in the 1970s.

Widespread deforestation is likely to be having a heavy impact on the numbers of these cats, particularly on the island forms such as *Neofelis nebulosa diardii*, which occurs on Sumatra. Here, an estimated 65–80 per cent of the lowland forest has disappeared since the turn of the century. Although clouded leopards are still found in all eight of Sumatra's provinces, their distribution has become highly fragmented. This is likely to have serious implications for the species in the future, although it is now clear that it is not as dependent on forested habitats as was previously believed. In the Way Kambas Game reserve in Lampung province, clouded leopards have been observed in both grassland and mangrove swamps.

Six other species of wild cat can be found on Sumatra, and it is believed that differences in hunting techniques enable them to survive without coming into direct competition with each other. The Asian golden cat does hunt in trees, but takes smaller prey than the clouded leopard, which is thought to prey mainly on primates as well as birds. In some areas clouded leopards may also take domestic stock, such as cattle and pigs. Unfortunately, the widespread use on Sumatra of organochlorine poisons such as DDT, often in the vicinity of game reserves, represents a threat to these cats. Education of the local people, and possibly some form of compensation scheme, are needed to safeguard these and other cats from such persecution.

Distribution of the clouded leopard (*Neofelis nebulosa*).

Little is known about the habits of the clouded leopard (*Neofelis nebulosa*), which is a shy, forest creature.

Elsewhere, it may already be too late. It is thought that the Taiwanese race of the clouded leopard *Neofelis nebulosa brachyurus* is already extinct, hunted out of existence for its pelt. These are yellower than those from other parts of the species' range, and in the past were used for ceremonial garments. A recent investigation in southern Taiwan uncovered six such jackets, all of which were reputedly over sixty years old.

The apparent demise of the clouded leopard here has led to an increasing demand for skins from overseas, with pelts being smuggled into Taiwan illegally. These can sell for as much as 1500 US dollars, and are clearly likely to threaten the population in China itself. A crackdown on smuggling may help to restrict this market before it causes serious damage to surviving clouded leopards elsewhere.

Little is known from the wild about their breeding habits, but pregnant females become very secretive when they are about to give birth. Gestation lasts approximately thirteen weeks, with two or three cubs then being born. At this stage the blotches on the flanks are almost entirely black and lack the charactertistic lighter centres. Males grow significantly faster than females from six weeks onwards, and are heavier, weighing up to 22 kg (49 lb) when mature.

Snow leopard *Panthera uncia*

DISTRIBUTION
Restricted to localities within the mountainous areas of Central Asia, occurring in parts of the former USSR, India, China, Afghanistan and Himalayan countries.

The striking greyish fur of the snow leopard, with a yellowish tinge on the flanks and creamy-white underparts offset against dark rosettes with light centres and smaller black spots, give these cats an unmistakable appearance. Their eye coloration is also unusual, being greyish green. The head is relatively small, with rounded ears, and the short legs terminate in powerful, broad paws. The thick tail, which has a black tip, is almost as long as the body itself. It is used to provide a counterbalance when the snow leopard jumps, and also to give protection against the bitter cold – it is wrapped around the body when the cat is resting.

The snow leopard is frequently recorded above the tree level, at altitudes between 2700 and 6000 m (9000–19,700 ft). In some areas, they have been observed hunting in pairs, but this may simply be during the mating period. Snow leopards are crespucular in their habits, being most active in the early morning and again in the late afternoon. Their ranges frequently overlap, and they prefer to move down on to prey from higher ground, killing with a bite to the neck. Blue sheep (*Pseudois nayar*) are a major food item, but these cats will also take a variety of other animals including ibex, musk deer, marmots, hares and birds. Snow leopards are also known to attack domestic sheep and goats on

The snow leopard is sometimes known as the ounce, which is a corruption of its scientific name, *Panthera uncia*. It is a species which typically occurs at high altitudes.

163

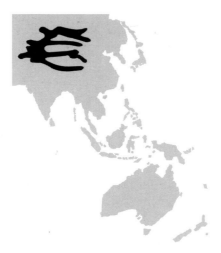

Distribution of the snow leopard (*Panthera uncia*).

occasions, which has led to conflict with local people, especially in the Altai range of Mongolia.

Since as many as a dozen snow leopards were being killed as a consequence each year, in 1986 the government decided instead to permit safari hunting, offering a maximum quota of five snow leopards. Each kill would cost the hunter 11,200 US dollars. The scheme has proved highly controversial. Its supporters suggest that it provides a basis to compensate the local people, and to prevent more widespread killing of these cats in this remote part of the world. All profits are intended to go to the livestock owners, and only known troublesome snow leopards may be shot.

It is estimated that the population of snow leopards in Mongolia lies between two thousand and four thousand, although other estimates consider that the total world population is only around five thousand. Poaching, especially in China, represents a serious threat to these cats. It has become an increasing problem as the number of tigers has declined: the bones of snow leopards are now substituted in traditional medications. The fur too is in demand. Unfortunately, human hunting of ibex and blue sheep, as well as poisoning of marmots, has tended to force snow leopards into greater conflict with people and the number of attacks on domestic livestock in China has increased. Although in theory the species has been protected here since 1983, enforcement is difficult.

In neighbouring Pakistan, however, good populations of snow leopard exist in the relative safety of the Khunjerab National Park. While some domestic stock is taken here, particularly in the winter and early spring, no serious attempt is made by the local people to curb snow leopard numbers.

These cats appear to have a relatively fixed breeding period, as might be expected in this harsh climate. Their cubs have the greatest likelihood of survival if they are born well before the winter snows. The female will retreat to a cave or similar den about a week before giving birth, which usually occurs between May and July. Her offspring, numbering up to four, are more intensely marked at this stage, and are born with a full coat. They will be weaned by three months old but stay with their mother for over a year, learning the hunting skills which are vital to their survival in this inhospitable environment. During the winter the family may move down to a lower altitude, to escape the worst of the weather and maintain their food supply.

Leopard *Panthera pardus*

DISTRIBUTION
Occurs over a wider area today than any of the other large cats, ranging across most of Africa apart from the Saharan region, through parts of Asia Minor and the Middle East eastwards to India, Pakistan, China, Siberia, much of mainland south-east Asia and the islands of Java and Sri Lanka.

Distinguishable from the jaguar by virtue of its smaller head and less stocky appearance, the leopard can also be recognized by the distinctive markings on its coat. Although both are rosetted in shape, those of leopards do not have the additional black spots in each rosette which characterize jaguars. The ground colour of a leopard's fur may vary from shades of yellow through to reddish brown. Melanistic leopards, often referred to as 'black panthers', are known; so are albinos, but they are much rarer.

Distribution of the leopard (*Panthera pardus*).

The highly adaptable nature of the leopard has enabled it to survive, at least in the African part of its range, without suffering a serious decline in numbers, in spite of the huge growth in the human population. Indeed, increases have been recorded in some countries, such as Zaire.

The leopard's lifestyle is a direct reflection of its environment, and in Africa's national parks they have become sufficiently bold to show themselves during the day. Elsewhere, in areas where they are likely to be persecuted, leopards are much shyer and essentially nocturnal.

These cats like a very wide variety of prey, being truly opportunistic in their feeding habits. They will catch and eat anything from insects and rodents up to large ungulates such as giraffe calves, which may weight 90 kg (about 200 lb). In areas where scavengers such as hyaenas could be a problem, larger kills are hauled off the ground into trees, but otherwise the carcass may simply be dragged into undergrowth.

In some cases, however, leopards are met with fierce resistance, as in the Tai Forest in the Ivory Coast where they attack chimpanzees. In one episode the apes were observed to chase the leopard down a narrow hole and trap it here. It roared consistently, trying to intimidate them, but members of the group threatened it with fallen branches, driving it back whenever it tried to escape. Finally, the group withdrew and the leopard retreated to safety. On other occasions leopards were seen to kill chimpanzees here, but in the majority of cases they were driven off, either by the chimpanzee itself or by others drawn to the area by their companion's alarm calls. Baboons have been known to act in a similar fashion towards leopards, with members of the troop driving them off and even killing them occasionally. Lions also kill leopards, as may tigers.

There has been considerable dispute over estimates of leopard numbers in recent years; most specialists believe that a computer prediction of a population of 700,000 in sub-Saharan Africa is a considerable over-estimation. They may, however, still be numerous here, but that is certainly not the case where individual Asiatic races are concerned. Severe habitat loss and human persecution have brought the Amur leopard (*Panthera pardus òrientalis*) to the verge of extinction. This race used to occur in the eastern provinces of the former USSR and neighbouring parts of China, with movements occurring in either direction across the Amur and Ussuri Rivers during the winter when these waters were frozen. When a survey was carried out here in 1972–3 only a maximum of twenty-five resident Amur leopards, and up to forty-six migrant leopards, were to be found. The situation worsened progressively, and the erection of an international border fence blocking the migration route of roe deer (*Capreolus capreolus*) meant that no leopards have been seen crossing the Ussuri River since 1984. The population had then fallen to a total of twenty-five to thirty.

Captive breeding has therefore been vital, and may yet prove to be the salvation of these leopards. Their coat patterning is particularly distinctive, being quite unlike that of other races. It has large, widely spaced rosettes with thick and usually complete borders. Concern has been expressed that some of the captive-bred individuals are not of pure lineage and have diluted the strain. Now, however, the authorities in the former USSR are planning to use some of the juvenile leopards which are leaving the area where they were born to establish a separate breeding programme near Ussurisk in Siberia.

Meanwhile, safe territories are being increased, and study schemes involving

Stealthy by nature, the leopard (*Panthera pardus*) has now become more evident in areas where it is largely free from persecution. As a result, in many of Africa's national parks, it is usually much more conspicuous than elsewhere, to the delight of tourists.

surplus male leopards from zoos will be set up in areas where these cats were once relatively common. There are even plans to develop tourism, as a means of raising funding for these projects and possibly to attract overseas backing. This is not the only race of leopard in the former USSR whose status is critical, however; the population of the Anatolian leopard (*Panthera pardus ciscaucasia*) is thought to have fallen to just a small number of individuals in the wild.

Mating in the northern part of their range, including eastern Siberia, occurs in the first two months of the year, taking place in the Caucasus slightly later. Up to four cubs may be born in a concealed den. Their fur is longer and has a more woolly texture than that of an adult leopard, while the markings are poorly defined at this stage. They will start to gain their adult coat at four months, separating from their mother when they are between eighteen months and two years old.

Jaguar *Panthera onca*

DISTRIBUTION
Extends from southern Mexico down through Central America and as far south as Paraguay, northern Argentina and possibly Uruguay.

The range of the jaguar has constricted considerably in recent years. It used to occur as far north as the USA, in parts of Louisiana, Texas and New Mexico. The last recorded specimen in California was killed in 1860, though the species survived in Texas and Arizona at least until the 1940s. It may have extended right down to the Magellan Straits at the tip of South America. The jaguar is a powerfully built, relatively stocky cat with short legs. As a further point of distinction from the leopard it has spots in the centre of its rosette markings. Melanistic jaguars have been recorded on occasions from various parts of South America, and possible albinos, with white claws, are also known. Males are significantly larger than females, averaging 55 kg (122 lb), but much heavier individuals, weighing as much as 136 kg (300 lb), have been recorded from the Pantanal area of Brazil.

Jaguars like to roam close to rivers and lakes, and are often found in areas of tropical forest where there is water nearby, but they may also be found in more arid upland areas where water is available. These cats are strong swimmers, and often appear to enjoy entering the water. They may catch fish here, as well as otters and caimans. Their powerful canines allow them to puncture even the protective shell of river turtles (*Podocnemis expansa*), which nest on exposed sand bars during the dry season. Jaguars will often excavate the eggs and eat them before they hatch. Snakes too may fall victim to these cats, including the feared anaconda, which itself often lives close to water.

Although occasional attacks on people have been recorded, it appears that jaguars rarely molest people and, unlike the leopard, do not develop man-eating tendencies. Their powerful canines, however, are quite adept at crushing the skull of their prey, which is often their favoured method of killing, and they are formidable predators – they take animals up to the size of a tapir (about the same size as a small pony) as well as peccaries, on a regular basis.

The jaguar (*Panthera onca*) is a regular reptile killer, whose ancestors have been preying on tortoises, turtles, crocodilians and lizards for as long as two million years. Fossilized turtle shells reveal past evidence of the fatal impact of jaguar's teeth.

Distribution of the jaguar (*Panthera onca*).

One of the most detailed surveys undertaken into the status of the jaguar through its range concluded in 1987 that the species is declining, especially in Central America, because the joint pressures of agriculture and development are leading to loss of habitat. The species had previously suffered severely from over-exploitation for the fur trade, although less recently than the small spotted cats from Central and South America. There were very few skins being traded by the mid-1970s when CITES came into existence, and the species was then accorded endangered status.

In some parts of its range, however, the jaguar is reasonably numerous; in Bolivia, for example, it occurs on the large ranches and sometimes takes farmstock. Yet these cats are not keen to cross fences erected to protect domestic animals. Where problems have occurred, the majority of jaguars involved are male. Studies have been carried out in Belize in Central America by Dr Alan Rabinowitz to see if translocating problem jaguars could reduce this type of predation, but it seems that the cats may start heading back towards the area where they were orginally caught. Once they have started to kill cattle, such behaviour can become habitual.

Working in the Cockscomb Basin in the southern-central area of the country, Rabinowitz discovered that here armadillos, along with deer, form a significant portion of the jaguar's normal diet. Since these studies in the early 1980s, this area has become the world's first jaguar preserve. Its 390 sq km (150 sq miles) are believed to be home to as many as forty jaguars. Although they are living at a relatively high density, communication by means of scrapes and faecal remains prevents unexpected confrontations.

When the breeding period starts, as many as eight males may be drawn to a single female. She will then give birth to up to four cubs, whose coats will be longer than those of adults. Only a hint of the lighter areas within the centre of the rosettes is likely to be visible at this stage. The cubs attain adult coloration at about seven months, but may remain with their mother until they are nearly two years old.

Tiger *Panthera tigris*

DISTRIBUTION
Occurs in various separated localities through much of southern Asia, including India, Bangladesh, Nepal and Bhutan, extends westwards to Iran and eastwards via the former USSR into China. Also present on some Indonesian islands.

The appearance of these large cats is unmistakable, with their striped patterning extending down the sides of the body. The ground colour is quite variable, however, and may vary from a pale yellow through to reddish ochre, depending on the area of origin. The underparts tend to be white. The Siberian race (*Panthera tigris altaica*) is both the palest in coloration and the largest in size, weighing as much as 320 kg (700 lb), which makes these the biggest cats in the world.

Tigers can be found in a wide variety of environments, although they require adequate cover so they can ambush their prey – large herbivores – which must be available in the area. They are also rarely found far from water.

The size and potentially aggressive nature of tigers towards people, and particularly to farm livestock, has meant that their conservation, following decades

Distribution of the tiger (*Panthera tigris*).

of big game hunting, represents a particular challenge. At its core must be a policy to promote the understanding and enlist the assistance of local people. The aim of Project Tiger in India, set up in 1972, is to safeguard the future of the species in that country through a series of reserves and buffer zones to prevent direct conflict with people. It has adopted an ecological approach, not concentrating just on the tiger, as the name suggests, but aiming to protect habitat and thereby enabling other wildlife populations to regenerate in these areas. Already, the numbers of tigers in India is believed to have risen from 1800 when the project began to over 4000 today.

Other subspecies have not been so lucky. On the Indonesian islands distinctive races used to occur on Bali (*Panthera tigris balica*), before becoming extinct here around 1937, and on Java, where *Panthera tigris sondaica* was present in some numbers; these were the smallest races. Today the Sumatran race (*Panthera tigris sumatrae*) is struggling for survival. Fewer than eight hundred individuals are believed to survive in the wild, often living in isolated areas which will inhibit breeding attempts as the cats may not meet often enough to mate successfully. In 1983 a total of 157 Sumatran tigers was located at 51 zoos and similar institutions, with the aim of setting up a co-ordinated breeding programme. These

The Siberian tiger (*Panthera tigris altaica*) is now an endangered race. A commercial breeding centre has been established in China and it is hoped that in the eight years between 1992 and 2000 it will produce over 600 cubs. This will effectively double the world's current population.

The distribution of tigers (*Panthera tigris*) has declined dramatically during the past century, leading to the extinction of some races. India now remains the most westerly point of the tiger's range although, formerly, they extended further west.

tigers all derive from a foundation stock of eighteen, of which at least fourteen · originated from the wild, starting in 1937. In-breeding in the American lineage has been more pronounced than in the case of European strains, which began with thirteen of these animals, but within the latter population the level of mortality in the case of in-bred cubs is higher.

It is to be hoped that efforts to save the Sumatran tiger will not supplant the endeavours already made by zoos with the Siberian tiger (*Panthera tigris altaica*). The investment in such programmes is huge – the annual cost of feeding the worldwide captive population was estimated back in 1983 to be 1.2 million US dollars. But such expenditure is necessary since there are reckoned to be only three hundred surviving in the wild. The status of other races, too, is becoming critical – as, for instance, the South China tiger (*Panthera tigris amoyensis*). This could be the second mainland subspecies to be lost during the present century, following the extinction of the Caspian tiger (*Panthera tigris virgata*) in the 1970s.

Large numbers of South China tigers were shot from the 1950s onwards. The dramatic effects of hunting on these large, solitary cats are shown by the fact that there were probably fewer than one hundred surviving in the wild by 1977, when they were given protection. Further decline has since taken place, because these tigers are highly prized in China for medicinal purposes.

Conflict with people has also been a major factor in their decline. Expanding settlements and agriculture in eastern and southern-central parts of China have removed much of the habitat which was suitable for the tigers; they are now restricted to the more inaccessible mountainous areas of country. This race has fewer stripes than any other subspecies, enabling it to be distinguished from the other races which occur in this country.

The latest figures suggest that there are probably more Chinese tigers in zoos than there are left in the wild, where the population appears to have plummeted to fifty or less. Captive breeding is clearly vital if these tigers are not to become extinct, which would signal the demise of half of the world's subspecies in barely fifty years. In the wild, protection not only of the remaining tigers, but also of their habitat and prey species, is equally essential to ensure its survival here.

In Siberia tigers breed during the spring, but in other parts of their range births may occur at any time. Males may often sustain bad cuts when fighting for a female, and on one occasion a tiger was observed packing the wound by rolling in damp mud – presumably to reduce the risk of it becoming infected. The female also drives the male away after mating, and this too can result in injury.

Pregnancy lasts up to 106 days, and as many as seven cubs may sometimes be born, although three or four probably form the average litter. They suckle for six months, being moved by their mother at intervals from one locality to another during this period. The cubs will finally become independent when they are between eighteen months and two years old. Aside from human hunting pressure, tigers have few natural enemies, and may live, at least in captivity, for well over twenty years.

Lion *Panthera leo*

DISTRIBUTION
Occurs in scattered localities across Africa south of the Sahara, extending as far south as Botswana. A tiny population of lions can still be found in Asia, within the relative safety of the Gir Forest Sanctuary in the west of India.

The range of the lion has contracted dramatically over the centuries. It used to occur from the southern shores of the Mediterranean right down to the tip of Africa, and westwards through the Middle East as far as the Bay of Bengal in northern India. The divergence between the African and Asiatic populations of lions took place between 50,000 and 200,000 years ago, according to genetic studies.

Although still common in parts of India in the 1850s, lions were considered to be nearly extinct here by the 1890s. The species disappeared from Tunisia at this stage, and had already almost vanished from Algeria as well. Its last stronghold in North Africa was the Atlas Mountains. Here, the last wild Barbary lion (*Panthera leo leo*) was shot in 1922, although it is clear that some hybrids may still be represented in zoological collections. This race was not only one of the largest, but also one of the most spectacular: mature male lions had a very large and prominent mane which extended over half the body, reaching the underparts and the middle of the back.

At the other end of Africa, the Cape lion (*Panthera leo melanochaitus*) met a similar fate. It too had a profuse mane, which in this instance was black. The

The lion is the only member of the family to display a prominent mane, present in mature males. According to cave paintings however, this may be a relatively recent development, not recorded in the case of the ancestral cave lion. This individual is a very rare Asiatic lion (*Panthera leo*). The tiny population of lions still surviving in Asia is now restricted to the Gir Forest region of western India

precise range of this subspecies was never documented, but it was last seen in Cape Province in 1858; the last known example was killed in Natal seven years later.

Lions are adaptable animals, but they tend to inhabit more open areas of country than most other cats; and since they occur in groups, known as prides, they are probably more vulnerable to hunting pressures. A further tragedy in the history of the lion occurred in 1991 within the Skeleton Coast Park in Namibia, which has an area of 15,000 sq km (5800 sq miles). Within the confines of this arid strip of land, bordering the Atlantic Ocean, a unique development had taken place – the lions hunted on the beach itself. They would scavenge, and also adapted to hunt the fur seals found here; a lion would drag one of these creatures, which can weigh up to 190 kg (about 420 lb), away from the safety of the sea and up the beach.

Since the park bordered an area of farmland these lions were always vulnerable to being shot, for fear they might attack livestock. This sadly proved to be the case, and all but one member of this unique group has now been killed by Herero farmers. It is not considered possible to repopulate this area now, even if

175

Distribution of the lion (*Panthera leo*).

the villagers could be persuaded not to shoot the lions, simply because any introduced lions would not have the necessary expertise to survive within the confines of this harsh environment.

In other areas where stock raiding has been a problem it has proved possible to move the lions to a region where natural game is more plentiful; indeed, two had been previously taken from the Skeleton Coast. When a lion has become conditioned to hunting farmstock, however, it can be virtually impossible to break this habit. There is also a risk that it may cause other members of the group to adapt to this type of hunting.

In Asia, there has been considerable recent in-breeding in the tiny remaining group of lions, which have a typical distinctive fold of belly skin. They are believed to total no more than 250, although it does appear that their population is continuing to rise slowly. These lions could so easily have been wiped out at the turn of the century when Lord Curzon, then Viceroy of India, was asked to take part in a shoot; at this time their population was thought to be just a dozen. But the Viceroy declined, and the Nawab of Junagadh gave the animals protection. The Gir Forest Sanctuary was set up in 1966 to prevent conflict as far as possible between farmers and lions. A small captive-breeding population of Asian lions is also in existence, and the future of this race appears reasonably secure.

It is planned to develop wildlife tourism in this area, as is taking place elsewhere in the world. Lions are inevitably a popular sight with tourists, attracting visitors from all around the world to countries such as Kenya. Eco-tourism is seen as a means of supporting the vast tracts of land needed to maintain viable populations of these and other cats. Lions generally have declined in numbers outside the boundaries of national parks, confirming the vital role of these areas in preserving this species.

Lions are very adaptable in their feeding habits; the females do most of the hunting, and prefer to do so in the early evening. Working in groups, they can overcome relatively large animals such as giraffes in relative safety. They sometimes approach prey from different angles. At other times lions will drive the

The Barbary lion (*Panthera leo leo*) is now extinct in the wild although attempts are being made to recreate this North African population in zoos, where the genes still survive in some lions, as the result of past hybridization between different races.

quarry towards other members of the pride which then ambush the game. They will scavenge when necessary, and even feed on insects and grass if other food is in short supply. Although adapted to a terrestrial life, these cats may occasionally climb trees.

There is a fairly fixed breeding season, with the adult males in the pride mating with the females and driving off any rivals. Females themselves may breed until they are at least fifteen years old. After a pregnancy lasting as long as 119 days, the female goes off and gives birth on her own to up to seven cubs. She usually chooses a den quite close to water for this purpose. When the cubs are about three weeks old and ready to start walking the lioness and her family rejoin the pride. The cubs will suckle not only from her, but also from other lionesses which are lactating, for six months. They then start to learn to hunt with other members of the pride. Mortality is high, and over half the cubs are likely to die within the first year, sometimes from starvation and sometimes as a result of attacks from male lions, hyenas, hunting dogs and other cats such as leopards. The surviving young males are driven out of the pride by the time they are two years old and start to wander on their own before fighting to take over another pride.

Cheetah *Acinonyx jubatus*

DISTRIBUTION
Now restricted to an area south of the Sahara in Africa, with just tiny populations surviving at various localities in North Africa and the Middle East.

Built for speed rather than for cautiously stalking and ambushing prey, the cheetah has a light body, weighing on average just 65 kg (about 145 lb) and distinctively long legs. Its coloration is yellowish with black spots, becoming paler on the underparts, while the tail is ringed towards its tip.

Distribution of the cheetah (*Acinonyx jubatus*).

The cheetah (*Acinonyx jubatus*) is the fastest mammal in the world, capable of sprinting at speeds up to 100 kph (62 mph) over short distances.

The cheetah's range has contracted significantly in recent years. Its distribution used to extend throughout Africa and eastwards to India in historical times. In Asia particularly, cheetah numbers have declined seriously, to the extent that it only occurs here in Iran and possibly Turkey as well as Turkmenistan. The centre of its distribution is now southern Africa.

Even here, however, their future may not be secure, since they face increasing opposition from farmers. In Namibia, which has one of the world's largest surviving populations, currently estimated at between two and three thousand, some farms lose 10 per cent of their calves to cheetahs. Overall, farmers have estimated the cost to the cattle industry to be about 2 million rand (approximately £430,000) per annum. There is a further problem in that the wild game upon which the cheetah also preys is not subject to hunting prohibitions. The farmers now view this as an additional source of revenue – cheetahs themselves are protected and therefore valueless, aside from occasional trophy hunting and a small number of exports of skins and live animals. No compensation is apparently paid for losses inflicted on farmstock by cheetahs.

The most recent studies carried out in Iran, one of the few remaining areas for cheetahs in Asia, suggest that the species is actually increasing its range here, at least in the province of Khorasan. This follows a period of falling numbers because of widespread hunting of gazelles, their major prey, as well as hunting of the cheetahs themselves.

In the past, cheetahs were widely kept in India especially. Here, the father of the Moghul Emperor Jahangir kept a thousand cheetahs for hunting purposes, and bred them successfully. This was documented by Jahangir in 1613 as a rare event in captivity; indeed, it appears to be the only record up until 1956, when

Philadelphia Zoo in the USA succeeded. Jahangir also described a white cheetah which he had been shown in 1611. Its white body had a slight bluish tone, and its markings were blue rather than black.

The difficulty encountered in breeding cheetahs stems from the fact that they barely cheated extinction at the end of the last Ice Age some ten thousand years ago. Up until this stage in history they had been very widespread, and then their numbers declined dramatically. Only a handful survived, and all today's cheetahs are descended from this tiny ancestral stock. Study revealed that male cheetahs had both a low sperm count and a significant proportion of abnormal spermatozoa, with the result that conception rates were seriously low. Further investigations then showed that there was very little genetic diversity in the entire population. This reproductive problem was the result of millennia of in-breeding, with adverse genes becoming increasingly dominant in the population as a whole. The situation extends to the immune system too, with the result that cheetahs are, for example, very susceptible to feline infectious peritonitis (FIP). Overall they are still at risk from their lack of genetic diversity, but inter-breeding between the races may improve the likelihood of their long-term survival.

Even when they are born, cheetah cubs face a hazardous time. In Tanzania, studies in the Serengeti National Park have shown that their mortality can be as high as 90 per cent in the first three months of life. Females may give birth to litters of up to eight, making them the most prolific of the wild cats. They go to great lengths to protect their cubs, moving them from one locality to another in order to disguise their presence. The young grow a characteristic mane, which starts to appear in about their third week of life remains evident until they are a year old.

The cubs split off and go their own way when they are about fifteen months old. Antelope, especially gazelles, form a major part of their diet, but hunting skills need to be learnt and refined. It may take three years for a cheetah to develop into a proficient hunter.

The density of cheetahs is relatively low, even where conditions are favourable. In Namibia, for example, there may be only a single cheetah in 50 sq km (20 sq miles) on average, with home ranges extending up to 1500 sq km (nearly 600 sq miles) in the case of females.

Onza (not yet classified)

The distribution of this species is unknown, although it is thought to be centred on the province of Sinaloa which runs down the western coast of Mexico. For many years the very existence of this cat was not suspected, in spite of the fact that the earliest records of it date back to the days of the Spanish invasion in the early sixteenth century; one of the conquistadors described the two types of 'lion', one of which was known as wolf cat and called *cuitlamiztli* by the Aztecs. To the Spaniards it became known as the onza – a name derived from the word *uncia*, which was used to describe the cheetah.

A number of subsequent reports followed, including one by Father Pfefferkorn, a Jesuit priest, who described the onza as having a long, thin body rather reminiscent of a puma, but with a bolder nature. This similarity to the puma meant that such accounts were essentially dismissed by zoologists, and no serious attempt was made to look for the onza.

Then, in 1938, a banker on a hunting trip, accompanied by two experienced hunters, shot and killed an onza in the upland area of San Ignacio district in Sinaloa. They could not identify the cat, but photographed and measured it, returning with the skull and skin. Unfortunately, their claim to have located a new species of cat was met with derision and the skull was lost in a museum. It has yet to be discovered again, in spite of an intensive search. Another obtained at about the same time did come to light, however, in Philadelphia's Academy of Natural Sciences.

Richard Greenwall, secretary of the International Society for Cryptozoology, continued his search for remains of the onza in Mexico, where in 1985 he traced the skull of a specimen shot in the mid-1970s. By this time, there was considerable debate as to whether the onza could be directly descended from the fossil Pleistocene puma, which was known as *Acinonyx trumani*. Greenwall disproved this hypothesis on the basis of the skull material which had been assembled, but it is possible that these forms could still be related.

A remarkable piece of luck then followed. It was on the night of 1 January 1986 that a rancher called Andres Murillo saw what he initially thought was a jaguar poised to attack him. He shot the cat, and was surprised to discover that it was neither a jaguar nor a puma. Having previously met Manuel Vega, who had been helping Greenwall in Mexico, and knowing his interest in unusual cats, Murillo contacted him.

Immediately an operation was begun to preserve the carcass and carry out a thorough investigation into the onza and its possible relationships with other members of the cat family. The specimen which Murillo had shot was a female, wieghing 27 kg (60 lb), in good body condition and significantly lighter than a puma of equivalent size. The body measured 113 cm (45 in), with the tail contributing an additional 73 cm (23 in) to its length. The cat had eaten recently – the remains of deer were found in its stomach.

At the present time further investigations are being made, including biochemical studies which are providing a genetic profile of this cat. Its precise taxonomic state is unclear; it could be related to the pumas which also occur in this region, or it may yet be shown to be a species previously unrecognized by zoologists.

No more specimens have since been reported, but a rather similar puma-like cat was said to have been hit and killed by a car on the border between Mexico and Texas in the 1950s. Its body then passed to the University of Texas, and the skeleton may still be stored in the collection there. Clearly, whatever the onza proves to be, it is a shy and nocturnal cat, having been elusive for so long.

Checklist of Species

Taxonomy of the species and subspecies within the family Felidae is somewhat controversial, and this checklist is based on both the taxonomic proposals put forward by Hemmer (1978) and those of Honacki et al (1982).

SUBFAMILY FELINAE

European wild cat
Felis silvestris silvestris
Felis silvestris caucasia
Felis silvestris euxina
Felis silvestris grampia
Felis silvestris molisana
Felis silvestris morea
Felis silvestris tartesia

African wild cat
Felis lybica lybica
Felis lybica brockmani
Felis lybica cafra
Felis lybica caudata
Felis lybica foxi
Felis lybica griselda
Felis lybica iraki
Felis lybica issikulensis
Felis lybica koslowi
Felis lybica matschiei
Felis lybica murgabensis
Felis lybica nesterovi
Felis lybica ocreata
Felis lybica ornata
Felis lybica pyrrhus
Felis lybica rubida
Felis lybica sarda
Felis lybica tristami
Felis lybica chutuchta
Felis lybica vellerosa

Domestic cat
Felis catus

Sand cat
Felis margarita margarita
Felis margarita airensis
Felis margarita meinertzhageni
Felis margarita thinobius
Felis margarita scheffeli

Jungle cat
Felis chaus chaus
Felis chaus affinis
Felis chaus fulvidina
Felis chaus furax
Felis chaus kelaarti
Felis chaus kutas
Felis chaus nilotica
Felis chaus oxiana
Felis chaus prateri

Black-footed cat
Felis nigripes nigripes
Felis nigripes thomasi

Chinese desert cat
Felis bieti

Serval
Felis serval serval
Felis serval beirae
Felis serval brachyura
Felis serval constantina
Felis serval hamiltoni
Felis serval hindeio
Felis serval ingridi
Felis serval kempi
Felis serval kivuensis

Serval *continued*
Felis serval lipostica
Felis serval lonnbergi
Felis serval mababiensis
Felis serval robertsi
Felis serval togoensis

Pallas's cat
Felis manul manul
Felis manul ferruginea
Felis manul nigripecta

Leopard cat
Felis bengalensis bengalensis
Felis bengalensis borneoensis
Felis bengalensis chinensis
Felis bengalensis euptailura
Felis bengalensis horsfieldi
Felis bengalensis manchurica
Felis bengalensis trevelyani
Felis bengalensis javaensis
Felis bengalensis minutus
Felis bengalensis sumatranus

Rusty-spotted cat
Felis rubiginosa rubiginosa
Felis rubiginosa phillipsi

Fishing cat
Felis viverrina

Iriomote cat
Felis iriomotensis

Flat-headed cat
Felis planiceps planiceps

African golden cat
Felis aurata aurata
Felis aurata celidogaster
Felis aurata cottoni

Asian golden cat or Temminck's cat
Felis temmincki temmincki
Felis temmincki dominicanorum
Felis temmincki tristis

Bay cat or
Bornean red cat
Felis badia

Jaguarundi
Felis yagouaroundi yagouaroundi
Felis yagouaroundi ameghinoi
Felis yagouaroundi cacomitli
Felis yagouaroundi eyra
Felis yagouaroundi fossata
Felis yagouaroundi melantho
Felis yagouaroundi panamensis
Felis yagouaroundi tolteca

Ocelot
Felis pardalis pardalis
Felis pardalis aequatorialis
Felis pardalis albescens
Felis pardalis maripensis
Felis pardalis mearnsi
Felis pardalis mitis
Felis pardalis nelsoni
Felis pardalis pseudopardalis
Felis pardalis pusea
Felis pardalis sonoriensis
Felis pardalis steinbachi

Margay
Felis wiedii wiedii
Felis wiedii amazonica
Felis wiedii boliviae
Felis wiedii cooperi
Felis wiedii glaucula
Felis wiedii nicaraguae
Felis wiedii oaxacensis
Felis wiedii pirrensis
Felis wiedii salvinia
Felis wiedii yucatanica

Little spotted cat,
oncilla or tiger cat
Felis tigrina tigrina
Felis tigrina guttula
Felis tigrina pardinoides

Geoffroy's cat
Felis geoffroyi geoffroyi
Felis geoffroyi euxantha
Felis geoffroyi leucobapta
Felis geoffroyi paraguayae
Felis geoffroyi salinarum

Kodkod
Felis guigna guigna
Felis guigna tigrillo

Pampas cat
Felis colocolo colocolo
Felis colocolo braccata
Felis colocolo budini
Felis colocolo crespoi
Felis colocolo garleppi
Felis colocolo pajeros
Felis colocolo thomasi

Andean mountain cat
Felis jacobita

Puma
Felis concolor concolor
Felis concolor acrocodia
Felis concolor anthonyi
Felis concolor araucana
Felis concolor azteca
Felis concolor bangsi
Felis concolor borbensis
Felis concolor browni
Felis concolor cabrerae
Felis concolor californica
Felis concolor capricornensis
Felis concolor coryi
Felis concolor costaricensis
Felis concolor cougar
Felis concolor greeni
Felis concolor hippolestes
Felis concolor hudsoni
Felis concolor improcera
Felis concolor incarum
Felis concolor kaibabensis
Felis concolor mayensis
Felis concolor missoulensis
Felis concolor oregonensis
Felis concolor osgoodi
Felis concolor pearsoni
Felis concolor felis
Felis concolor schorgeri
Felis concolor stanleyana
Felis concolor vancouverensis
Felis concolor olympus
Felis concolor soderstromi

SUBFAMILY PANTHERINAE

Caracal
Lynx caracal càracal
Lynx caracal algira
Lynx caracal damarensis
Lynx caracal limpopoensis
Lynx caracal lucani
Lynx caracal michaelis
Lynx caracal nubicus
Lynx caracal poecilictis
Lynx caracal schmitzi

Eurasian lynx
Lynx lynx lynx
Lynx lynx dinniki
Lynx lynx kozlowi
Lynx lynx isabellina
Lynx lynx sardiniae
Lynx lynx stroganovi
Lynx lynx subsolanus
Lynx lynx wrangelli

North American lynx
Lynx canadensis

Spanish lynx
Lynx pardinus

Bobcat
Lynx rufus rufus
Lynx rufus baileyi
Lynx rufus californicus
Lynx rufus escuinapae
Lynx rufus fasciatus
Lynx rufus floridianus
Lynx rufus gigas
Lynx rufus pallescens
Lynx rufus peninsularis
Lynx rufus superiorensis
Lynx rufus texensis
Lynx rufus uinta

Marbled cat
Pardofelis marmorata marmorata
Pardofelis marmorata charltoni

Clouded leopard
Neofelis nebulosa nebulosa
Neofelis nebulosa brachyurus
Neofelis nebulosa diardii
Neofelis nebulosa macrosceloides

Snow leopard
Panthera uncia uncia

Leopard
Panthera pardus pardus
Panthera pardus ciscaucasia
Panthera pardus delacouri
Panthera pardus fusca
Panthera pardus japonensis
Panthera pardus jarvisi
Panthera pardus felis
Panthera pardus melanotica
Panthera pardus nimr
Panthera pardus orientalis
Panthera pardus panthera
Panthera pardus pernigra
Panthera pardus saxicolor
Panthera pardus sindica
Panthera pardus tulliana
Panthera pardus adersi
Panthera pardus antinorii
Panthera pardus ehui
Panthera pardus dathei
Panthera pardus ituriensis
Panthera pardus kotiva
Panthera pardus melas
Panthera pardus millardi
Panthera pardus nanopardus
Panthera pardus shortridgei
Panthera pardus suahelica

Jaguar
Panthera onca onca
Panthera onca arizonensis
Panthera onca centralis
Panthera onca goldmani
Panthera onca hernandesii
Panthera onca palustris
Panthera onca peruvianus
Panthera onca veracrucis

Tiger
Panthera tigris tigris
Panthera tigris altaica
Panthera tigris amoyensis
Panthera tigris corbetti
Panthera tigris sondaica
Panthera tigris sumatrae
Panthera tigris virgata
Panthera tigris balica
Panthera tigris lecoqui

Lion
Panthera leo leo
Panthera leo azandica
Panthera leo bleyenberghi
Panthera leo hollisteri
Panthera leo massaicus
Panthera leo melanochaita
Panthera leo persica
Panthera leo roosevelti
Panthera leo senegalensis
Panthera leo somaliensis
Panthera leo verneyi
Panthera leo goojeratensis
Panthera leo krugeri

UNDETERMINED

Cheetah
Acinonyx jubatus jubatus
Acinonyx jubatus hecki
Acinonyx jubatus ngorongorensis
Acinonyx jubatus raineyi
Acinonyx jubatus soemmeringii
Acinonyx jubatus venaticus

Onza
Awaiting taxonomic placing

Further Reading

Although a number of titles in this list are out of print, they should be available from a specialist natural history book dealer, or possibly from a public library.

Adamson, George (1987), *My Pride and Joy*, Simon and Schuster, New York.

Adamson, Joy (1960), *Born Free*, Collins-Harvill, London.

Alderton, David (1983), *The Cat*, Macdonald, London.

Alderton, David (1992), *Eyewitness Handbook: Cats*, Dorling Kindersley, London.

Amman, Katherine and Karl (1985), *Cheetah*, Arco, New York.

Association of British Wild Animal Keepers (1991), *Management Guidelines for Exotic Cats* ABWAK, Bristol.

Bedi, Ramesh and Rajesh (1984), *Indian Wildlife*, Collins, London.

Bertram, Brian (1978), *Pride of Lions*, Dent, London.

Best, George A., Edmond-Blanc, F. and Whiting, R. C. (1962), *Records of Big Game (Africa)*, Rowland Ward, London.

Bottriell, Lena G. (1987), *King Cheetah*, E. J. Brill, Leiden, Netherlands.

Burton, John A. and Pearson, Bruce (1987), *Collins Guide to Rare Mammals of the World*, Collins, London.

Burton, Reginald G. (1933), *The Book of the Tiger*, Hutchinson, London.

Cahalane, Victor H. (1947), *Mammals of North America*, Macmillan, New York.

Clutton-Brook, Juliet (1987), *A Natural History of Domesticated Animals*, Cambridge University Press, Cambridge.

Corbett, Jim (1956), *The Man Eating Leopard of Rudraprayag*, Oxford University Press, London.

Corbett, Jim (1979), *Man Eaters of Kumaon*, Penguin, Harmondsworth.

Day, David (1981), *The Doomsday Book of Animals*, Ebury Press, London.

Denis, Armand (1964), *Cats of the World*, Houghton Mifflin, Boston.

Earton, Randall L. (1973), *The World's Cats*, Wildlife Safari Publications, Oregon.

Eaton, Randall L. (1982), *The Cheetah*, Krieger, Florida.

Ewer, R. T. (1973), *The Carnivores*, Weidenfeld & Nicolson, London.

Francis, D. (1983), *Cat Country: The Quest for the British Big Cat*, David & Charles, Newton Abbot.

Grzimek, H. C. (1984), *Grzimek's Animal Life Encyclopedia* Vol. 12, Van Nostrand Reinhold, New York.

Guggisberg, C. A. W. (1963), *Simba: The Life of the Lion*, Chilton Books, Philadelphia.

Guggisberg, C. A. W. (1975), *The Wild Cats of the World*, David & Charles, Newton Abbot.

Halstead, L. B. (1978), *The Evolution of the Mammals*, Peter Lowe, London.

Haltenorth, Theodor and Diller, Helmut (1980), *A Field Guide to the Mammals of Africa including Madagascar*, Collins, London.

Imaizumi, Y. (1976), *Report on the Iriomote Cat Project*, Environment Agency, Tokyo.

Jackman, Brian (1982), *The Marsh Lions*, Elm Tree Books, London.

Kingdom, J. (1977), *East African Mammals* Vol. 3A, Academic Press, London.

Kitchener, Andrew (1991), *The Natural History of the Wild Cats*, Christopher Helm, London.

Kurtèn, Björn (1971), *The Age of Mammals* Weidenfeld & Nicolson, London.

Leopold, Aldo S. (1959), *Wildlife of Mexico*, University of California Press, Berkeley.

Leyhausen, Paul (1979), *Cat Behaviour: The Predatory and Social Behaviour of Domestic and Wild Cats*, Garland STPM Press, New York.

Loxton, Howard (1973), *The Beauty of the Big Cats*, Ward Lock, London.

Loxton, Howard (1990), *The Noble Cat: Aristocrat of the Animal World*, Merehurst, London.

McBride, C. (1977), *The White Lions of Timbavati*, Paddington Press, London.

McBride, C. (1981), *Operation White Lion*, Paddington Press, London.

Macdonald, David, ed. (1984), *The Encyclopaedia of Mammals*, Geroge Allen & Unwin, London.

McEwan, Graham J. (1986), *Mystery Animals of Britain and Ireland*, Robert Hale, London.

McFarland, David, ed. (1987), *The Oxford Companion to Animal Behaviour*, Oxford University Press, Oxford.

McNeely, Jeffrey, A. and Wachtel, Paul S. (1988), *The Soul of the Tiger: Searching for Nature's Answers in Exotic South-east Asia*, Doubleday, New York.

Matthews, L. Harrison (1969), *The Life of Mammals* Vol. 1 and 2, Weidenfeld & Nicolson, London.

Matthiesson, Peter (1978), *The Snow Leopard*, Viking, New York.

Mountford, Guy (1987), *Wild India*, Collins, London.

Necker, Claire (1970), *The Natural History of Cats*, A. S. Barnes, New York.

Pallas, Peter Simon, ed. Carol Urness (1967), *A Naturalist in Russia: Letter from Peter Simon Pallas to Thomas Pennant*, University of Minneapolis Press, Minneapolis.

Patterson, John H. (1907), *The Man Eaters of Tsavo*, Macmillan, London.

Pease, Alfred Sir (1914), *The Book of the Lion*, Scribner, New York.

Pocock, Reginald I. (1951), *Catalogue of the Genus* Felis, British Museum (Natural History), London.

Rabinowtiz, Alan (1986), *Jaguar: Struggles and Triumphs in the Jungles of Belize*, Arbor House, New York.

Rudnai, Judith, A. (1973), *The Social Life of the Lion*, Medical and Technical Press, London.

St George, E. A. (1987), *A Guide to the Gods of Ancient Egypt*, Spock Press, London.

Savage, R. J. G. and Long, M. R. (1986), *Mammal Evolution – An Illustrated Guide*, Facts on File, New York.

Schaller, George B. (1967), *The Deer and the Tiger*, University of Chicago Press, Chicago.

Schaller, George B. (1972), *The Serengeti Lion*, University of Chicago Press, Chicago.

Schaller, George B. (1973), *Golden Shadows, Flying Hooves*, Alfred Knopf, New York.

Scott, Jonathan (1988), *The Leopard's Tale*, Hamish Hamilton, London.

Seidensticker, John and Lumpkin, Susan, ed. (1991), *Great Cats, Majestic Creatures of the Wild*, Merehurst, London.

Shuker, Karl P. N. (1989), *Mystery Cats of the World*, Robert Hale, London.

Shuker, Karl P. N. (1991), *Extraordinary Animals Worldwide*, Robert Hale, London.

Singh, Arjan (1973), *Tiger Haven*, Macmillan, London.

Singh, Arjan (1984), *Tiger! Tiger!* Jonathan Cape, London.

Tabor, Roger (1983), *The Wildlife of the Domestic Cat*, Arrow Books, London.

Thapar, Valmik (1986), *Tiger: Portrait of a Predator*, Collins-Harvill, London.

Tilson, Ronald L. and Seal, Ulysses S., eds. (1987), *Tigers of the World*, Noyes Publications, New Jersey.

Tomkies, Mike (1991), *Wild Cats*, Whittet Books, London.

Whyte, Hamish, ed. (1987), *The Scottish Cat*, Aberdeen University Press, Aberdeen.

Young, Stanley P. and Goldman, Edward A. (1946), *The Puma: Mysterious American Cat*, American Wildlife Institute, Washington DC.

Useful Addresses

The Cat Specialist Group
IUCN Species Survival Commission
International Union for the Conservation of Nature
World Conservation Centre, Avenue du Mont-Blanc
1196 Gland
Switzerland
Members receive *Cat News*, published twice annually, which contains details of
the latest research on wild cats of all species.

International Society of Cryptozoology
PO Box 43070
Tucson
Arizona 85733
USA
Members receive a quarterly newsletter and the annual scientific journal
Cryptozoology. Concentrates on more esoteric aspects of cat research, breaking
new ground with reports of the discovery of the onza.

Cat Survival Trust
Marlind Centre
Codicote Road
Welwyn
Hertfordshire
AL6 9TV England

The Ridgeway Trust for Endangered Cats
PO Box 29
Hastings
East Sussex
England

The above two organizations are concerned with the survival of all felids,
particularly the smaller species.

Index

Page numbers in *italic* refer to black and white illustrations. Page numbers in **bold** refer to colour plates.